ONCE
A
BITCOIN
MINER

ALSO BY ETHAN LOU

Field Notes from a Pandemic:
A Journey Through a World Suspended

ONCE A BITCOIN MINER

SCANDAL AND TURMOIL
IN THE
CRYPTOCURRENCY WILD WEST

ETHAN LOU

Published by ECW Press
665 Gerrard Street East
Toronto, Ontario, Canada M4M 1Y2
416-694-3348 / info@ecwpress.com

Cover design: David A. Gee

LIBRARY AND ARCHIVES CANADA CATALOGUING IN
PUBLICATION

Title: Once a bitcoin miner : scandal and turmoil
in the cryptocurrency wild west / Ethan Lou.

Names: Lou, Ethan, author.

Identifiers: Canadiana (print) 20210177675 |
Canadiana (ebook) 20210177691

ISBN 978-1-77041-539-3 (softcover)
ISBN 978-1-77305-588-6 (ePub)
ISBN 978-1-77305-589-3 (PDF)
ISBN 978-1-77305-590-9 (Kindle)

Subjects: LCSH: Lou, Ethan. | LCSH:
Cryptocurrencies. | LCSH: Bitcoin. | LCSH:
Currency crises.

Classification: LCC HG1710.3 .L68 2021 | DDC
332.4—dc23

This book is funded in part by the Government of Canada. *Ce livre est financé en partie par le gouvernement du
Canada.* We also acknowledge the support of the Government of Ontario through Ontario Creates.

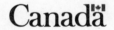

PRINTING: FRIESENS   5   4   3   2   1

completecure.me

CONTENTS

PROLOGUE

Jonathan Edwards rarely saw the neighbors across the street, but now he wondered if one day he'd be walking by and see a shooting right out front. What about his three-and-a-half-year-old boy? Why were lawmen storming that house? And just three days before Christmas! Jonathan did not know. But he did know this: he'd moved there for a reason. There, outside the city, you could watch your horse run for miles on the flat prairie grass and not see a single other person, but when you stopped your car by the side of the road, out of nowhere would come a helpful voice asking if everything was okay. There, people drew their curtains before sundown. The local gas station closed at 10 p.m. Jonathan had sought the hamlet for its bigger lots and tranquility. He had moved, in part, because nothing at all was supposed to happen there.

That night, inside the McMansion across from Jonathan, the sin was stacked black and high with weapons and drugs, and the 25-year-old gangster Real Honorio and four others were hauled away by the law under the waning crescent moon. Real would come to regret the pain and anguish his crimes caused, the sordid chapter of his life so mired in gunfire and blood he had been blind to what was important. As a boy, Real had been interested in art and had a sense of justice, having won the local newspaper's Superhero Stamps contest by designing his own character, Flame Thrower. Now everything had culminated in the death of a dream, as Real's parents would describe, shame and brokenness to his whole family.

But that came only much later, after Real was arrested again, charged with and convicted for a different deed. Ten days after the December raid, Real was out on bail, and into his mind cantered the pale thoughts of death, fair and frigid like the falling snow. Revolver in hand, Real and his fellows stormed a Vietnamese restaurant. Muzzles flared amid the eatery's white lace curtains and aquariums filled with colorful fish, and two rival outlaws dropped to the ground, bleeding. The acrid smell of powder filled the air, bullet holes marred the green walls, and empty shell casings bounced upon the reddening floor. Keni Su'a, a construction worker eating at the restaurant, ran out the door. He did not see the steely gun sights that stalked him.

Once married to a local doctor, Keni was a Pacific Islander who had first crossed the salty sea to North America to spread the good word of Jesus Christ. Keni had come to love the cleanliness of the New World, the warmth of its people, and what he had seen as its safety. Described as humble and gentle and with a great smile, Keni went to the restaurant often, and on that New Year's Day he faded away in the frost outside, bleeding out between the snowbanks, the bright crimson flowing where no such color should ever be. For a moment, almost imperceptible, a faint vapor would have risen from Keni as his warmth was lost to the brittle air. Keni never learned why he was damned to die that January 1 of 2009, age 43, in Calgary in western Canada, in the bleak early winter, 6,000 miles from the island he had once called home.

Those who spend enough time on the internet may come across the term "sonder," coined by the online linguistics project the Dictionary of Obscure Sorrows to describe the realization that "each random passerby is living a life as vivid and complex as your own — populated with their own ambitions, friends, routines, worries, and inherited craziness — an epic story that continues invisibly around you like an anthill sprawling deep underground." In those stories, "you might appear only once, as an extra sipping coffee in the background, as a blur of traffic passing on the highway, as a lighted window at dusk." And those moments are the faint links between different worlds, snaking through every look and every touch and every shoulder brushed. We hardly notice those links, and even when we do, we can never fully appreciate the strangeness of their paths or the complexities of the stories to which they lead.

There is no easy answer as to why Keni died that New Year's Day. It was Real's .357-caliber revolver, and his finger on the trigger, but the islander was not his target. Real had mistaken him for a rival outlaw. The two did not know each other and shared nothing other than their presence in the restaurant that afternoon. Keni died simply because he was there, because the other restaurant he had wanted to visit was closed, because he'd picked the wrong day to crave Vietnamese food. Leaving his homeland of Samoa to preach the gospel, Keni had been the protagonist of his own epic, but that afternoon, he was nothing more than an unwitting, unfortunate extra, sipping tea in the background of Real's life.

As Keni lay dying, the restaurateur Dan Dang hid in the freezer. She had not seen the bullets fly, but she had heard their murderous thunder, and she was both cold and scared. Later, Dan saw the victims on the floor. One was on his stomach, bleeding from his mouth. A young woman held the body and cried. That scene had come from a gang feud that Dan had done nothing to invite, about which she knew little and cared even less. What Dan did know, though, was her own story. She had fled a troubled Vietnam and endured the brutal high seas only to end up in a Malaysian refugee camp before finding a new life in North America. Dan screamed in her sleep that night. The restaurant had been the culmination of more than a decade's toil in a local meat plant by her and her husband, who had also been a refugee. Now Dan didn't think she could ever go back. Meanwhile her husband worried that, with yellow police tape sealing off the place, there was no way to put food into the aquarium and that the fish were dying.

Two days later, on January 3, 2009, Bitcoin was introduced into the world, and in that same sonder-esque way that people silently pass through each other's lives, through those elusive links that meander between worlds, all that turmoil of the December raid and the New Year shooting, all that sorrow and pain, that destructive convergence of all those dissimilar lives, would be connected to a new story, albeit faintly — no more than a fleck of paint in the backdrop of an entirely different play.

ACT I

2013 HIGH: $1,200

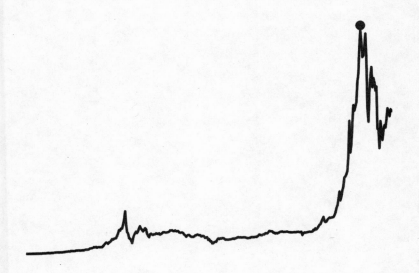

CHAPTER 1

I grew up in Wuppertal in western Germany, the birthplace of both aspirin and heroin, invented by the same guy in a two-week period in the nineteenth century. My childhood began a little after the fall of the Berlin Wall, and my doctoral-candidate father supported the family on the modest income typical of his position. I remember when he hauled home an old bicycle for me, all the way from another city. I hated it and never rode it. I think it used to belong to a girl. The plastic decorations on the spokes were too pink, and like the hand-me-downs I wore, the bicycle was too big.

When I turned eighteen, it was in a job market battered by the 2008 financial crisis, a milestone marked by need and uncertainty. Banks had increasingly profited by offering risky mortgages to those who should not be getting them, and then building complicated investment products on top of them. When those borrowers couldn't repay, that triggered an avalanche in the interconnected financial system, and people around the world lost homes, jobs, and retirement savings. That same year, a faceless figure known only as Satoshi Nakamoto released a nine-page white paper, made with off-brand software: "Bitcoin: A Peer-to-Peer Electronic Cash System." Whoever was behind that pseudonym, that person or group had been fueled and driven by the financial crisis. In Bitcoin's first batch of transaction records, dated January 3, 2009, called the Genesis Block, Satoshi Nakamoto encoded a message that directly referenced that sordid affair. The creator cited a *Times* of London article about a potential second government bailout for the banks. Billions were to be spent helping the usurers — again — to rescue them from a storm of their own making. And that storm had spewed forth something: Bitcoin was spawned from an opposition to the financial status of the world, a frustration against the same bleakness that had surrounded me my whole life. It was, perhaps, natural that eventually it would pull me in — although probably not in the way that Satoshi Nakamoto had intended.

I first heard of Bitcoin in my second year of university, but I can't remember if it was 2012 or 2013. My friends Dillon and Clinton can't remember either. It's been too long, and there is a non-zero possibility we had too much marijuana that day. Clinton has the worst recollection: "Don't think I was there."

I was in university in Toronto, in Canada, where I studied journalism. We three were at Clinton's city-subsidized apartment in a building full of drug dealers and hoarders, a place described by a newspaper columnist as "freakishly menacing and macabre" due to the frequent mysterious deaths there. We were on the dark web that day, the internet's uncharted armpit, for a reason commonly behind the questionable decisions young men make, not unlike the reason people risk their lives to climb tall piles of rock or ride raging farm animals just to see how long they can stay atop.

The dark web is unmapped by mainstream search engines and accessible only through special software, most commonly a browser called Tor. The dark web has many legitimate uses, but it is more well known for the illegitimate ones. If you can imagine something — anything — then it can be found on the dark web. Al-Qaeda and pedophiles and all forms of the grotesque have lurked on its pages. My friends and I stumbled upon the term "vore" and clicked on a related link, only to discover it meant cannibalism porn. We did not linger long enough to see if it was real or staged. Elsewhere on the dark web, various marketplaces offered stolen credit card details and passwords, drugs, and guns. You could also hire someone to say the right words to police so that a tactical team would raid a house of your choice, a process called "swatting." My friends and I even found purported assassinations on offer — just unbelievable.

Whatever the service or product, those dark web entrepreneurs required payment in Bitcoin. Not long after its release, the world's first cryptocurrency had seen its first major use case. Like the BitTorrent file-sharing protocol, Bitcoin operates through a network of its users, without a central administrator. All the dark web transactions were theoretically outside any government's reach. I could not help but feel that held some sort of broader value, even if I could not exactly place it, and I soon revisited the subject.

After that year of university, I spent the summer interning at a newspaper in Saint John on Canada's east coast, an economy so decimated that, on my way in, the taxi driver was surprised I was in town for a job. I made $15 per hour, $10 less than at big-city newspapers such as the *Toronto Star*, where my application was among the hundreds rejected.

It was in Saint John that I interviewed over the phone a Bitcoin advocate for an article: Anthony Di Iorio, founder of what was then known as the Bitcoin Alliance of Canada, a late-thirties alumnus of my university, a serial entrepreneur who previously dug geothermal boreholes and operated rental housing, among other ventures.

It's hard to explain Bitcoin to people, Anthony said. "You get what I call the Bitcoin stare, where people look at you a little bit weird."

But explain traditional money to people, and you often get the same reaction. The two are actually quite similar. Consider the Micronesian island of Yap, which had once used large, donut-shaped stones as currency that the people dubbed "rai." Because they were heavy, the rai stones themselves didn't actually change hands. People simply agreed the ownership had changed, as if there were a ledger tracking all the stones. So the actual stones became less important. At least once, a stone was somehow lost, but it continued to be traded as if it still existed. The figurative ledger had become the actual currency system. In a fundamental way, that's how all money works, just records on ledgers. What makes Bitcoin different, though, is that its ledger, called a block-chain, is distributed among its network and governed entirely by code, making it theoretically impossible for any one party to forge a transaction, go against pre-defined rules, or otherwise control it.

As seen with the dark web, that feature was useful, and with a limited quantity hardwired into Bitcoin's code, supply and demand had driven up its price, kind of like a stock. The creator Satoshi Nakamoto had meant for Bitcoin to be a medium of exchange, but it moved more wildly than any currency from a functioning economy. "It's grown more in value than anything else," Anthony said matter-of-factly. Bitcoin's first known real-world transaction had been 10,000 units for two pizzas in 2010, an abysmally low per-coin valuation that quickly became outdated. "I mean, when I first purchased," Anthony said, "I got in at around $10, and it's gone up as high as $250." By the time we spoke, Bitcoin was hovering around $100, but there was still a certain confidence in Anthony's speech, the kind that belongs to the sinewy sort of man who seems competent in a poker game. "It will grow much higher. I think, eventually, it's going to be up in the thousands."

Bitcoin's properties had implications for everything from monetary policy to geopolitics. But for all the wider potential that Anthony saw, my personal takeaway from our conversation was the price movement. I could not stop thinking about how much Anthony had made as I walked home that day to my rental apartment void of furniture, in an aging city where all the young were moving away, where, right in the middle of downtown, for the first time in my life, I saw an actual bingo hall. "The thousands!" I thought as I passed the discount supermarket's rusting trash bins, which inexplicably bore cheery slogans such as "Smile," "Enjoy life," and "Never give up." They spewed forth the whiff of expired milk that, damp with the ocean air, smelled just like cheese.

CHAPTER 2

Later in the summer of 2013, I got a call from the *Toronto Star*. I was finally going to work in that gray, waterfront monolith that had been voted by one-fifth of the newspaper's own readers as the ugliest building in the city. But faced with declining revenue, the *Star* had considered eliminating that internship program, and when I skipped the first day of my third year of university and walked into its concrete eyesore, I was taking a one-third pay cut from what had been offered to the previous year's interns. It was pretty close to what I had made at the east coast paper. That was not unique, not to internships or even to the media world. The job market everywhere was decaying, even as universities pumped out more graduates. I was keenly aware that I was among the lucky ones.

A month later, I tried LSD for the first time with my buddy Dillon, with whom I had earlier discovered the dark web, in his little room in a shared house. I lived in one of those places, too. Mine cost some $500 per month, and the streetlamps shone right through my windows, and hookah smoke kept creeping in from the hazy den downstairs. It was the hallmark of student life, even as many lived there long after graduation. Dillon and I unwittingly took three times the standard dosage and followed Bilbo Baggins across Middle-earth's vast and lawless plains in the film *The Hobbit*. In terms of the original books, I've always loved *The Hobbit* more than the related *The Lord of the Rings*. The former I read as an adult, but the latter when I was no more than thirteen years old, when I understood little and retained even less, perusing it in part because I wanted people to see me flipping through a big book and assume I was smart and beyond my years for reading such a big book. Watching *The Hobbit* with Dillon, what drew me in especially was the sullen dwarf, Thorin, bitter and lonely after years of wander, who never so much as unfrowns until the end. "The young dwarf prince took work where he could find it," Bilbo says in the opening narration. Thorin is on a quest seeking enchanted gold and a home — "you don't have one," Bilbo later tells him. That day, that resonated in me with an intensity that wrung my heart.

In many ways, my generation considered itself damned. In the United States, young adults were half as likely to own a home as their counterparts in 1975. More than half of millennials with student loans had delayed major life events, such as marriage or having children, because of their debt. Full-time employment for Canadian men between 17 and 24 had fallen by almost a quarter over the past 40-some years. In the United Kingdom, those problems were causing millennials to be the first generation to have worse health than their parents. While looking up those numbers, I also read that a male millennial's fertility would have been irreversibly damaged by age eighteen because of all the processed modern junk food in the average diet. It didn't have much to do with the economy, but it made me sad all the same to learn that, on top of everything, there was something wrong with the fundamental function of me and my fellow men.

So when the end of the year came, and Anthony Di Iorio's Bitcoin price prediction turned out to be right, it was as if the fates had whispered something important, and only I was listening. Bitcoin, once cheaper than half a can of bacon grease, had touched what was then an all-time high of more than $1,000. As I sat in the *Toronto Star* offices, I wondered how many millions Anthony must have made. Outside, the winter wailed.

Years later, I would tell part of this story to Anthony. I even told his parents, when I unexpectedly ran into them. But I don't think I ever got across to Anthony the journey that he sent me on. We were not and would never become close acquaintances. I was just an extra in the background of his life.

I took the plunge that December day. So excited was I, I gave small portions of my Bitcoin purchase to my parents as belated Christmas presents and excitedly extolled to them the currency's virtues. "This is the future of money," I said, channeling Anthony. "It's bound to go up."

It wasn't long before I started cursing Anthony, his matter-of-fact confidence and "toned physique and aloof manner," as one newspaper would later describe.

Unknown to me, trouble stirred in the Bitcoin world, and it was wild, and it was heavy. Japan's Mt. Gox, the world's largest platform for buying and selling Bitcoin, perhaps the one major brand in cryptocurrency the mainstream knew at the time, was collapsing like a dead star, and the weight of it all would ripple. Less than three months after I'd bought Bitcoin on that fateful New Year's Eve, the currency had fallen 50 percent from what was then its all-time high. What the hell had I been thinking? I vowed to sell all my bitcoins and never touch the cursed currency again.

Of course, I did neither.

Run by Mark Karpeles, a plump Frenchman in Japan with kind eyes and an easy smile, Mt. Gox let users deposit traditional currency to buy Bitcoin from each other or vice versa. The name was short for "Magic: The Gathering Online eXchange," as the site had originally been intended to be a platform for trading collectible cards. Naturally, the mainstream finance world still viewed Mt. Gox as such. It did not help that Karpeles, who looked really silly in a Reuters interview sitting inexplicably on a blue exercise ball, was like many Bitcoin early adopters. Young men more geek than entrepreneur, they were ironically uninitiated to the red tape and clunky inner workings of finance that crypto-currency was purported to solve, yet that which an exchange could not avoid. Accused of frequently boasting of his high IQ and prioritizing the needs of his cat over attending industry events, Karpeles soon began to feel the weight of finance jargon like "compliance," "know your customer," and "money services business." In 2013, the U.S. government seized some of Mt. Gox's funds. Banks shunned it. Users could not withdraw their money. Then came the revelation of what Karpeles described as hacking attempts that had stolen nearly $500 million of Bitcoin over the years. Karpeles showed up uneasily in a gray suit at a Japanese news conference. His long, dark hair looked like it was slicked down with gel for the first time. He bowed before he spoke. "We have lost bitcoins due to weaknesses in the system," Karpeles said in Japanese. No doubt, he tried to keep his face neutral, but he was one of those people whose resting expression was gentle and friendly, almost like a smile, like Private "Gomer Pyle" in *Full Metal Jacket*. "We are really sorry for causing trouble to all the people concerned." And so Mt. Gox went bankrupt.

For a product whose dollar-value swings solely on supply and demand, that scandal had torpedoed the price, analysts said. By the summer of 2014, Bitcoin had bounced back just a sliver to $600, a little more than half of the height from which it fell. It was a price pitiful, yet also heavy.

There was, as well, the social price. The thing about embracing cryptocurrency is that once you go down that path, you become "that guy," the one who explains Bitcoin to all your friends, the one who springs to mind when they chance upon the topic. "Oh, Bitcoin? I know a guy who has some." Every gathering, every party, I was quizzed about my investment.

"Oh, I'm doing fine," I would say with a chuckle, to show I was doing fine. "You know what they say, never gamble with money you're not prepared to lose. Haha."

Beneath the armor, I was gashes and gore. It wasn't that much money. I wasn't stupid enough to play with funds I needed to pay bills or buy food or anything. And I had had an upgrade in my internship, ascending to $25 per hour. But what had gone into Bitcoin was all of my savings. I floated month to month untethered, one bad day away from blood seeping through mail and plate and into the open. Sometimes, when nobody was looking, I swear all I did was stare into the distance, as if I had lost a brother to pneumonia.

Then there were my parents, to whom I had given Bitcoin for Christmas. I'm sure they'd read the news of the fall. Yet they never brought it up. Those coins I gave them hung like some Greek sword over every weekly video-call session, like that incriminating, Vaseline-lubricated carrot in the Chuck Palahniuk short story "Guts" that a character's mother stealthily takes from his room and then never mentions again. I started to dread the video calls — did my parents believe they'd sired a simpleton who pissed away everything on worthless internet-scrip monkey money?

"God, our son's a jackass," they must have thought, "just a mistake or two away from becoming Carrot Boy."

It was a long summer — the sort that stretched and stretched and faded into time itself — in my tiny apartment above the hookah place, where I claimed a decisive yet hollow victory against bed bugs, and where an eyebrowless neighbor with severe mental-health issues constantly tried to hit on me. Sometimes when I looked out the window that summer, silently resentful of all creation, it was as if I could see the world standing still.

The person I least wanted to see was Anthony Di Iorio, so naturally, I would meet him in person for the first time.

CHAPTER 3

Anthony was clad in a white T-shirt that matched his office's white décor, which made the place look bigger. He had started a software company, Decentral, and held regular cryptocurrency meetups, setting up shop in a redbrick house in Toronto's historical fashion district.

"I saw your article," Anthony said, without further comment.

I had interviewed him earlier for a piece I was writing, and he had invited me to one of his gatherings, which were posted on Meetup.com, a site with a self-explanatory name. "The most challenging part was trying to summarize what Bitcoin is in one paragraph," I said, before instantly regretting it.

"Really?" Anthony lit up. "I want to hear this." Maybe he hadn't read the article that closely after all.

I stammered out a few lines that were nowhere near as eloquent as I thought they would be.

About a dozen young men attended the meetup, dressed casually but also deliberately. The walls were lined with glass whiteboards. Soft drinks and potato chips were put out for the attendees, although the latter were of a boring flavor, like lightly salted or barbecue. I didn't tell Anthony I had lost money on Bitcoin. I did not want to sound stupid.

There was a presentation by Bitwage, which offered a service that allowed companies to pay their employees with cryptocurrency. I had been working on another cryptocurrency article, about that very subject, to coincide with Labor Day, and at that event, I met several people who were taking salaries in Bitcoin.

One was Gerald Cotten, a bright-eyed, sandy-haired 20-something whose face, like that of Mt. Gox's Frenchman Mark Karpeles, had a gentle resting expression. Gerry had founded the exchange platform QuadrigaCX, where people could buy and sell cryptocurrency. He is, of course, most famous for being declared dead in India and sending shockwaves across and beyond the cryptocurrency world. But on the day we met, it was still the simpler time of 2014.

A business-school graduate, Gerry was a fixture in Toronto's growing cryptocurrency scene, attending Anthony's meetups even before the latter had secured his fashion-district building. Reserved, private, and an avid player of Settlers of Catan, a nerdy strategy board game, Gerry avoided gluten and drank cider, eschewing beer due to digestive problems.

Gerry shook my hand and handed me a black business card — white text upon a dark, perforated steel theme. It was nice-looking, but it was clearly not made by a professional. There were at least three different fonts on it.

I knew Gerry a little by reputation. At the time, there were few platforms in Canada where you could buy and sell crypto-currency easily, in an organized fashion, with local currency. Everyone knew Gerry and Quadriga. "Aren't you in Vancouver?" I asked.

"Oh, no," Gerry said. "We were, but we just moved to Toronto."

I asked Gerry about Quadriga. It was then only nine months old, and it wasn't doing that well. Only some $7 million worth of Bitcoin would trade hands on the platform that year, and it would take in only about $20,000 in revenue from November 2014 through January 2015, against almost four times that in losses.

Yet Gerry had gone all in. "I make all my money in Bitcoin," he said. He seemed in for the long haul, a steadfast believer in the future of cryptocurrency.

For a while, I almost forgot about all the money I had lost. There was something oddly inspiring about Gerry. I decided to hold on to my Bitcoin. So it crashed even further, at one point going below $200.

You would expect that I would have grasped my lesson by then and gotten out. As they say in the *Warrior* television show, in a line that I will never forget because of the sheer cruelty it evokes, even a blind dog learns after being beaten enough. But if spicy food, roller coasters, and horror movies are any indication, we humans have a knack for choosing suffering over ease. Sitting in my tiny apartment, where a neighbor constantly hogged the communal bathroom to shave his head, I bought more Bitcoin.

Running through my head was, I suppose, the typical gambler mentality, thinking that if I kept playing, I could somehow recoup losses, that events came in patterns, and that after a string of bad luck, I would surely encounter better fortune. Then there was the general consensus of the scene. Everyone was confident Bitcoin would go back up. People earned entire salaries in it, after all. I, too, started seeing a little of what they saw, that Bitcoin's in-built scarcity and almost complete resistance to outside control held a certain value. As well, some who had entered the cryptocurrency space earlier remembered a worse decline in 2011, when Bitcoin tumbled to $2 from what had then been a high of $32. Imagine if you'd sold then. Imagine the weight of that regret. Cryptocurrency circles preach iron-faced stoicism and resistance to the urge to panic-sell, distilled into the meme of the mantra "HODL," a comical misspelling of "hold." Dramatic swings happen all the time, and when it falls, it means Bitcoin is on sale, as the belief goes. I bought Bitcoin on Gerald Cotten's Quadriga, and I went with the flow of HODL.

At the same time, after going to Anthony's meetup and getting to know Gerry, I had delved increasingly deeper into the cryptocurrency world, finding it endlessly fascinating. Because Bitcoin is open source, anyone can copy and repurpose its code. People had come up with hundreds of alternative cryptocurrencies, or altcoins, and were also applying Bitcoin's blockchain technology to uses aside from money. They were branching into separate, sometimes even rivaling domains, but also collectively forming a literal new world of crypto-blockchain, with its own industry, rules, and community. I started to realize there could be more to it than just dollar-profits.

I decided to spend bitcoins to see what practical use there was for the currency. The fact that one bitcoin was worth a couple of hundred bucks was no limitation on what you could buy with it. One coin is divisible to eight decimal places, so theoretically, you can buy a cup of coffee with Bitcoin. But at the time, there weren't many cafes accepting the currency. Most use cases for cryptocurrency were still of the unconventional variety. I made a losing bet on a gambling website against the boxer Floyd Mayweather when he fought his rival Manny Pacquiao, a mistake I repeated years later when the former took on the mixed martial arts fighter Conor McGregor. I also ordered ten hits of LSD for 0.412 bitcoins on the dark web.

I didn't habitually partake by any measure. But, that final semester of my journalism degree, I had somehow cleared most of my course load and had almost no classes, and it was a paralyzing winter with little to do. Moreover, I'd always believed the most important criterion for considering an activity was its novelty. Another one of my well-thought-out plans around that time, for example, was to attend the Pyongyang marathon in totalitarian North Korea, a place about which I had long been curious, and I had trained extensively only for the country to ban foreigners amid the Ebola outbreak. And while I did not pay it much heed back then, it was also around this time that the idea for this book first came to me. I'd long accepted that I was someone who would politely be called "eccentric." In 2018, when Changpeng Zhao — founder of what would be known as the world's biggest cryptocurrency exchange platform, Binance — talked about his company's operating model, it was as if he had cracked open my being and peered at my soul: "We have a very simple decision-making process and we don't really dwell on it. And once we [have] decided, we just execute. . . . If I make, like, 80 percent good decisions, it's usually okay, as long as the 20 percent decisions are not fatal."

The LSD purchase, though, would turn out to be a 20 percent decision. In retrospect, I should have seen that coming, for it had happened just two weeks after a dark day: North America's first rodent out of hibernation in the Groundhog Day event had caught a fright from its own shadow, scuttling back into its earthen burrow and, according to folkloric tradition, forecasting six more weeks of cold and frost. And I would learn a painful lesson. No LSD ever came in the mail. Because Bitcoin transactions are irreversible, my coins were gone for good. Such scams were common on the dark web, I later learned. In 2020, *Harper's Magazine* did a deep dive into the assassination market to find it was full of false hitmen. The more illegal your purchase, the more common the scams. The LSD dealer was anonymous, like almost everyone else on the dark web, and I had no way to pursue the matter.

Then I met Anthony again.

CHAPTER 4

By 2016, Mark Karpeles of Mt. Gox, accused of taking users' money for himself, had been arrested and thrown into a Japanese jail, from which he emerged far skinnier, yet no less emphatic in protesting his innocence — he was eventually cleared of embezzlement, convicted only on falsifying the exchange's data. I had graduated from university and had gotten hired by the international news agency Reuters. By then, Bitcoin's price had recovered slightly, but not by much, and I had long since chucked the matter out of my mind. Then I heard Anthony also had a new job.

While he still ran Decentral, Anthony had also become the new chief digital officer of the Toronto Stock Exchange, which was keen to explore potential uses for the blockchain technology behind Bitcoin. I ended up interviewing Anthony at his sparse office in downtown Toronto.

There in the financial district was where I also worked — just a block away, in fact. The area teemed with towers all glass and steel and inhuman, as if harsh houses built by heartless men. Every few blocks, centuries-old facades of buildings old as the city itself were tacked onto their modern successors. Toronto was rife with such juxtapositions, and critics called them jarring and ugly. But I'd always felt they had a certain charm, as if their mishmashes of present and past revealed a special connection between the two.

Anthony had been on the job for a little over a month, and he seemed reluctant to go into detail about his work, saying it was still in its early stages. "Everybody can see — they know my background and they know I've been hired here, and they can put two and two together." He added a cryptic note: "I'm here part-time, but I'm also here full-time."

Anthony's office was big and full of wood. It was largely empty except for the furniture and, on the tables, two bottles of water, a coffee cup, some paper, and one of those rare smartphones that still had a keyboard, which somehow I also used. Anthony's computer was on a desk behind his main one, suggesting he was the sort of important man whose days were spent talking to people instead of staring at a screen. Anthony himself looked oddly polished. Gone were the white T-shirts that had been his trademark. Now he wore a white button-down, albeit untucked, and glasses.

Rather than his stock exchange job, Anthony was more interested in talking about a new project. Nearly everything we do online relies on centralized servers holding all our information, big corporations overseeing all our activities. Think Facebook. Think gaming or banking. If a server gets hacked, a lot is lost. If Google reads your emails, you probably have no way of even knowing. We put a lot of trust into these central administrators. "That's retarded," Anthony said. But what if, through the blockchain technology behind Bitcoin, that can be different? A version of that idea can be traced to the same meetup where I first met Anthony in person. It was not his idea, but he had been among the first to hear it, and with his Bitcoin wealth, he had bankrolled the initial work on it.

Vitalik Buterin, an elongated Toronto young man who looked brainy in a very literal way, had attended Anthony's first meetup and later brought to him an idea for a blockchain platform he called Ethereum. It's a name that references the mythological fifth element ether, the pure essence that Greek gods breathed that was a building block of existence itself. Bitcoin was made to be a more democratized form of money. "Ethereum uses the same technology, basically, to create sort of a computing environment that you can use for pretty much anything," Vitalik told attendees at one meetup. He wore a whimsical T-shirt featuring the head of a cartoon character.

In the same vein as Bitcoin, the Ethereum platform was made to be decentralized, uncontrollable by any one party. Its core feature was the "smart contract," a sort of self-executing program. "That program can say if this particular condition happens, then send this amount of money to this person." Vitalik talked with his hands. "The program is just guaranteed to execute it according to whatever path you set." With that, the goal was to cut the central administrators from online applications and services, leaving only users interacting with each other, and code running practically by itself. Ethereum was to let people develop cloud storage without central servers that could be hacked, banking services without banks taking cuts, and social networks without a company reading your messages. Even new cryptocurrencies could be created, far more easily than before, Vitalik said. "You can make your own currency on top of Ethereum. A currency is basically just a program."

Anthony, who viewed Vitalik as a "very undersocialized kid," didn't know what to make of everything when he gleaned the concept. But Anthony saw potential, and he brought Vitalik's idea to the more technically savvy, and a core team of eight was gathered. The platform launched to overwhelmingly positive reception, although by the time Anthony and I spoke, he had already left the Ethereum project.

Ethereum intrigued me, but more interesting were Anthony and his new job. He did not view it as any sort of promotion or a legitimization of what he did or as any recognition by the mainstream finance world, which he did not covet anyway. Anthony didn't see himself as becoming part of a bigger body, but vice versa: the stock exchange gig was just one gear in his clock. In a way, it was the same with Vitalik, who had taken on the Thiel Fellowship, a program by the eponymous U.S. billionaire who co-founded PayPal, which paid young people $100,000 to skip or drop out of university to pursue other projects. These were not people searching for well-trodden paths in life but walking their own.

That was a peculiar notion that made me uncomfortable in a way, for I had been the exact opposite. It wasn't so much that I didn't want to forge my own path in life — I just didn't know what that was or where to begin. For as long as I could remember, despite my sometimes unconventional interests, I had always wanted to be a part of something, as if having a larger group stamped upon me would save me from having to find my own identity. I had at the time a job that was the envy of a lot of my friends, but was it truly what I wanted? That day, Anthony and I shared a silent elevator ride at the end of the interview. Neither of us can recall why exactly, but something had lingered in the air, unspoken but not unnoticed.

My job eventually moved me, first to New York City and, by the end of 2016, to Calgary in western Canada, the heart of the country's oil industry. Soon after I landed, the giant bronze head of a beaming old gold miner greeting me at the airport, two events happened that would make my mind drift back to that meeting with Anthony. One was a phone call with the man himself, when I was writing about him again. Ethereum has its own cryptocurrency, Ether, with which users pay transaction fees to run programs that operate on the platform and which can be publicly bought and traded. One ether had debuted at about 30 cents, but by the time Anthony and I spoke after I'd landed in Calgary, it had surged some 70-fold to touch $20. Unclear to me whether it was related or not, Anthony was leaving the Toronto Stock Exchange to focus on his own project: the Jaxx "wallet," which could hold multiple cryptocurrencies, uncommon at the time. "Jaxx really started taking off over the past months, and that's really where my passion is," Anthony told me. "I prioritize the things that are really important to me, and that's the number one thing."

The second event that made my mind wander back was the movement of the cryptocurrency market in general. I had checked prices after that call, and for reasons still mysterious to me, Bitcoin was on its way back to the $1,000 mark that it had hit in 2013. My losing investment was bouncing back. Almost three years to the day, I was finally going to be whole. Not only that, I was profiting from the Bitcoin I had bought at $200. When I'd arrived in the city — on vast prairies in the shadow of mountains, a land "to have great victories, to taste bitter disappointment," as its mayor had said — I chalked up my excitement as the routine sort brought on by any new development. But looking back, it was more than that. My life had been changed. I just didn't know it yet.

ACT II

2017 HIGH: $20,000

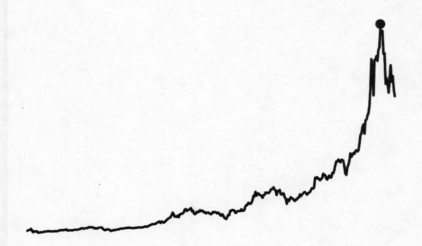

CHAPTER 5

People have lived around Calgary for millennia. But the modern city, like many in the North American west, has little history. Its earliest incarnation only appeared in the late nineteenth century, after Captain Éphrem-A. Brisebois, an American Civil War veteran, arrived in the area with 50 fellow redcoats from the North-West Mounted Police. Sent to quell the illegal whiskey trade, the group crossed the raging Bow waterway on a late summer day and commissioned a pine-and-spruce fort that would later become the city. Brisebois, a French speaker from the east, near Montreal, clashed with everyone around him and rode back alone. But his men stayed, among them a Constable George Clift King, who had been the first of them to set foot on the land, and who later became mayor. When King crossed that river, scarlet coat upon his back, at least a part of him felt that there was no going back. King would sometimes be called the city's "first citizen."

For the longest time, the settlement centered on that Mountie fort. There was a cattle boom, but it was only after the Second World War that the city truly prospered, eventually boasting more than a million people, after prospectors struck oil 170 miles north. But fortunes are fickle, and those tied to oil especially so. Boom-bust cycles abounded. When oil crashed in

2014, both in the city and in the Alberta province it's in, darkness fell on all alike, from executives downtown to roughnecks and camp cooks up north, from ranchers on the prairies to that military-garbed drifter I would later always see hanging around the financial district. Domestic abuse rates hit their highest in over ten years as husbands lost jobs. Eastern travelers seeking fortune turned their eyes homeward. Property prices plunged as a once-mighty region was brought low.

I arrived in town in the stillness after that storm. Just before my journey, Fergal, an Irish Reuters colleague who knew so much about economics and finance that I had to google every third word he said, had given me sage advice. "Ethan," he said, "buy a house," for houses were cheap there. Those words were never far from my mind as I arrived. "A house," I thought. I fondly remembered my last course in university, during which I read V.S. Naipaul's *A House for Mr. Biswas*, in which the titular character's perennial search for a permanent dwelling represents a far bigger, more personal quest for "his own portion of the earth." Fergal's was a most fitting piece of advice.

In the early twentieth century, North American governments were giving free land to anyone who wanted to settle in the West, in what they viewed as the unconquered frontier. With the subsequent economic booms, it remained a place to which many went in search of something in their lives. While I did not realize it immediately, I was definitely searching for something. With my investment in Bitcoin up and Anthony Di Iorio's phone call fresh in my mind, I watched as he, along with other fathers of Ethereum, became an even richer man, eventually worth up to a billion, according to *Forbes*. A curious thing had happened. The Ethereum project had raised funds for development by selling its Ether to the crowd. While an ether conferred no ownership stake, that process was otherwise just like selling a company's shares. It even had a similar name, the initial coin offering (ICO), and among all the facets of Ethereum, that was the one that had immediately caught the attention.

Ethereum was not the first to do an ICO, but because it was an all-purpose computing platform, it provided a foundation on which other projects could effortlessly issue their own coins and sell them to the public. So the market teemed with new digital assets, on top of the hundreds of already-existing ones. All of their prices usually went up and down along with Bitcoin's, but with even greater swings, and everything was surging at the time. A new boldness and a fresh hunger took hold of me. A restless want.

I had also been thinking about my time right before I arrived in Calgary, when I spent six weeks in New York. I covered the international oil markets and talked to professional traders daily, and that gave me deeper insight into how market forces influence a commodity's price and how to read the tea leaves of chart movements. Those traders actively bought and sold, profiting off price movements more so than just buying and holding the commodity. Cryptocurrency often made me think of those days. In terms of comparisons in the traditional markets for Bitcoin, gold is probably the best one, but black gold isn't too far off. Oil is traded largely on paper, without physical delivery, and its price fluctuations are considered volatile.

By then, my Bitcoin holdings had grown to be worth a princely $30,000. A wiser man, of course, would have sold all the bitcoins bought over the past three years and gotten out with no loss and even a little gain on top. It was only luck that had returned me my investment. If not luck, then certainly forces beyond my control. But I was on a roll, I thought. What would become of the man who spurned fortune, who turned his nose up at providence?

I let it ride.

I started trading, and I became obsessed with it. I checked prices constantly and had all sorts of alerts for different movements. Day and night, I traded.

I was attending a journalism conference in the picturesque mountains of Banff, Alberta. The national editor of the *Atlantic* had come all the way from Washington, D.C., to speak, and I had rented a car, driven more than an hour west to be there, and had paid hundreds of dollars for that privilege. But I wasn't listening. My head was down. The light from my phone disturbed those around me in that dark theater, but I didn't care. The charts showed Ethereum's Ether, by then the second-most-valuable cryptocurrency, was about to go up. I was in the process of buying several thousand dollars' worth of it.

I was at a gala dinner hosted by my alma mater. I mumbled unintelligible grunts to my date and ignored the others at my table. Bitcoin was going down, and I needed to sell.

I was at a grocery store checkout, I was waiting for a plane, I was watching a movie — it didn't matter. For conventional finance, the market closes after office hours. Mainstream traders can just switch off. For cryptocurrency, no such luck. The market runs 24/7, and you'd better, too. If at any moment in the day I did not have an internet connection and thus did not know what the price of Bitcoin was, I felt naked and vulnerable. Price determined my entire emotional spectrum.

First thing I did upon waking, even before the morning piss, I checked Bitcoin prices. If at any point in the night I woke up, I'd check Bitcoin prices. I woke up a lot. So engrossed was I, even at work, that I had an extra screen entirely devoted to cryptocurrency prices. Through trading, I started making money that rivaled my salary. Thus my new passion became even more intense. So all-engulfing it was, it carried a sort of break in the space-time continuum. Outside, the day could become night and the sky could rain ashes, and I wouldn't notice. I cut down on the mainstream news I consumed and filled the gap with cryptocurrency developments and price analyses.

That had a curious effect. Our perceptions of our surroundings are hardly objective. We form opinions and gain world views only through the information we process, the newsletters we read in the morning, the television we watch at night, and the podcasts we stream on the way to work. A 2020 *Financial Times* article investigated how Amazon's smart assistant Alexa curated the news it put out, questioning if it might unduly influence minds. We are the media we consume. Being a newsman, I have long curated my diet religiously. In fact, one of the many staple interview questions for a journalism job is "From where do you get your news?" When I changed that, it was as if I had changed, too, like some sort of slow-trickling cyberbaptism.

But while it seemed to me at the time that Bitcoin was eclipsing the other aspects of my life, pulling me away from them, the truth is more nuanced. I was growing restless at my job, perhaps in the same way all millennials just entering the workforce do — it was certainly an honest "it's not you, it's me" situation. It's possible I was going through some sort of quarter-life crisis. The other aspects of my life were already shrinking, and cryptocurrency had merely expanded into the resulting void.

Whatever the underlying reason, though, increasingly I became cloistered in the new world of crypto-blockchain. I started seeking out like-minded people.

CHAPTER 6

The airport inn was a drab series of brown and beige blocks, all designed by the same guy who planned all the other aviation-hub hotels. It was also named the same way, given some fancy-sounding moniker that on closer examination reveals itself to be utterly meaningless: the Executive Royal Hotel, which was later renamed just the Royal Hotel, presumably after its owner had a near-death experience and wanted to correct all the mistakes in his life.

I chained my bicycle outside, against a reedy young tree covered by red ants that were savoring their final freedom in the autumn air, before the cold would force them dormant beneath the soil. The wind blew, and with it, the branches whispered.

Something was off, and I knew that almost as soon as I arrived at the event that had been advertised as a cryptocurrency workshop on Meetup.com. I saw "iPro Network" plastered on the banners outside the hotel event hall, and I googled that unfamiliar name only to make a horrifying discovery: BehindMLM, a website that monitors scams, had linked iPro to the Bulgaria-based OneCoin, which had raised the wrath of authorities in the United States and more than a dozen countries in Asia and Europe after bringing in more than $4 billion. Often called a Ponzi or pyramid scheme, it had raised the money by selling what critics said was not even a real cryptocurrency and promising high investment returns that never materialized. While iPro's association with OneCoin was unproven beyond BehindMLM's allegation, I had gone to the hotel hoping to meet other cryptocurrency enthusiasts, and I started to feel it might not turn out to be the sort of event I had in mind.

I should have left immediately. But I had cycled more than half an hour to get to that inn by the airport, against a morning wind that gnawed my knuckles white. I was cold and hungry. I imagined glorious sizzling bacon and over-easy eggs whose membranes popped to release yolk still runny. Golden hash browns burnt just the right amount and with a splash of vinegar. Toast with crispy exteriors but soft insides that caved in like fresh snow. Earl Grey tea and just a dash of milk to turn it a nice silken brown. Maybe they would serve breakfast, I thought.

It was the stupidest decision of the year. Not only was there no food, but given that I had already sat down, packed into a phalanx of other attendees, I found it too awkward to just get up and leave. There would be way too many instances of "excuse me" I would have to say, way too many eyes in the room on my sorry person. I sat rooted, cursing my gluttony.

So I started recording with my phone, which I could do, both legally and ethically, because it was an event open to the public and Canada's relevant laws have what is called "one-party consent." I didn't know what I was going to do with the recording, but — looking back, rather presciently — I thought I might write about it in some form one day.

Among the half-dozen speakers at the hotel event hall was an ex–U.S. Marine, standing proudly and excitedly before the crowd of about 60. His name was Johnny Read, and he was a worldly man. "My other home is Thailand, and I've been there for the last ten years, so I'm surrounded by the Buddhist culture,"

Johnny said, seemingly without context, after he told everyone he had been a Marine. "I'm not Buddhist myself, but I studied Buddha. He was an incredible individual. And I get a different perception."

I didn't quite get what Johnny meant, but I took one look at him, and I instantly thought of Steven Seagal — the Marine wore the same type of gaudy Mandarin-collar suit favored by the Hollywood actor. Yet it wasn't so much the physical resemblance. It was everything else. I thought of the action-movie star Seagal and his claims of being some sort of mystic Buddhist master, advising U.S. intelligence operatives, and fighting Japanese mafia. It was evident these two were both very serious men. The difference was, of course, that Sergeant Johnny Ingram Read was not merely acting as a warrior. Later, when writing this book, I verified with the military that Johnny had served as a Marine Corps radio repairman and had earned an official commendation for helping bury 220 servicepeople killed in a suicide bombing in Beirut.

Johnny spoke from a temporary stage. It was the sort that could be quickly packed up and hauled away, leaving no evidence it was ever there, like how the circus comes and goes. "Mentoring is what this business is all about, listening to people that have" — Johnny raised his voice for emphasis — "already succeeded." The Marine continued: "The person I have the privilege of bringing up here is one of those such individuals. . . . He got involved in kind of what we're doing here, which is called" — his speech slowed to pronounce the next word, which he said with an upward inflexion — "cryptocurrency, just about three years ago, but now being [sic] a multiple seven-figure incomer."

Two standee banners flanked Johnny. One showed a smiling woman holding her credit card and looking at a laptop. The banner bore the logos of the major technology companies Amazon, Shopify, and eBay. While spokespeople from the former two did not respond when I asked, an official from the third was rather emphatic that "eBay does not have a relationship with this organization." The other banner featured nothing but vague, futuristic imagery in blue tint: a translucent globe merging from a smartphone held by a hand, with lines of computer code in the background. At the time, I still had little idea what iPro actually did.

"Wouldn't it be great to follow somebody who's making six figures a year?" Johnny asked. "I mean, that would be a safe thing to do, right? How about somebody who's making *multiple* six figures a year? But here, in this opportunity, he's making multiple six figures a *month* already."

Among the crowd was Dave Bradley, the city's cryptocurrency forefather, who had set up its first Bitcoin ATM — which isn't an ATM in the traditional sense but simply a terminal on which you can buy Bitcoin in person. Dave was an ursine man, with big forearms, whose face was all brown beard and glasses, constantly clad in a black T-shirt and jeans. I did not meet Dave that day, but he later told me he thought at the time that Johnny and his crew were pushing "some kind of Ponzi scheme." So Dave started saying that out loud, he recounted with a laugh. Dave was someone who thinks not just before he speaks but also while he speaks, like a politician at a press conference. Dave also had a bluntness, a certain no-frills, utilitarian approach to language that disregards fluff and flourish. The organizers promptly called security to kick him out, Dave said.

Bitcoin had been on a tear throughout 2017, quadrupling to almost $4,000 by the time of the iPro event. It had continued to reflect a broader appreciation of the entire cryptocurrency market, buoyed by Ethereum and the wave of ICO (initial coin offering) fundraising it had ushered in. Ethereum had the most fitting name. For the cryptocurrency folks, it was the very air we breathed, the conduit for the sun that warmed us. All sorts of investment money poured in for all sorts of coins and projects. Stories abounded of those making it big. Erik Finman, for example, from a little city in Idaho, became a millionaire at age eighteen, winning a bet with his parents that would allow him to skip university. Those stories showed possibility. If you had but known Bitcoin back in the day — think of where you would be now. So the name of cryptocurrency burst into the mainstream, for when hope catches on, it spreads like a prairie fire. It attracted hordes, even the techno-illiterati, seeking fast riches. So followed the snake oil salesmen and slipshod wildcatters, seeking the same.

The purported product of iPro Network was what it called its own cryptocurrency, which it said would be widely used in the future, thus ensuring its value, even though you couldn't do much with it at the moment. You made money by earning a commission when you persuaded people to buy into it through you, an operating model not that different from that of the infamous OneCoin.

Following Johnny Read was a fellow named Bob Byrum, the guy said to make "multiple six figures a month," a father of eleven, a bespectacled, pull-yourself-up-by-your-bootstraps kind of guy from the California city that gave the world the electric guitar. "Priorities — I just want to share with you what's happened in my life so that you know me a little bit," Bob said. "That is, putting God first, my wife second, my family third, and my business fourth." The next thing out of his mouth could have well been that he was on talking terms with every angel in heaven. Bob's 21-minute presentation meandered through how he couldn't pay rent in the past, but just that week, he and associates "rented three helicopters and flew through the Grand Canyon, just for fun." Bob showed a music video by his daughters and introduced his wife and a son whom he had brought along. He also contradicted Johnny, saying he got involved with cryptocurrency two years earlier, instead of three. He did everything except explain precisely how he'd made the money he was said to have. "You guys don't even know how special of a day this is for you," Bob said. Before playing his daughters' music, he read out the lyrics, "I'll take you to Neverland." He then quoted scripture, "Trust in the Lord with all your heart and lean not to your own understanding." I later tried to track down Johnny and Bob, to tell them I would write about them and to see what they had to say about all of this, but was unsuccessful.

R esearch shows most American students, from middle school to even university, can't tell news from propaganda. It would not be surprising if most people can't tell the difference between a legitimate crypto-blockchain project and a scam selling useless coins. Perhaps that was why shady operations were so rife. A 2017 article in the *Atlantic* was ominously titled "The Rise of Cryptocurrency Ponzi Schemes." In that Wild West of a world, there was little research on precisely how prevalent those questionable investments were, but in 2018, a user of the forum Reddit listed an alleged 104 of them. It was as if there were a great cosmic sausage-making machine, operated by some malevolent butcher-god, churning out links and links of these. Most notable was Bitconnect, whose coin crashed to below $1 from a high of nearly $500. The exaggerated sing-song mannerisms of its American promoter Carlos Matos — "Hey hey hey; hey hey hey; hey hey hey; wassa-wassa-wassa-wassa-wassa-wassa-wassa-wassup, Bitconnect!" — would become a meme, encapsulating the high-energy presentations, vague explanations, promised high returns, and dubious success testimonials for which such scams were known.

I left the iPro event during the lunch break, for the organizers did not serve lunch either. I was as hungry as when I'd arrived, and despite the friendly sun overhead, the wind was just as biting. Later that day, I spent $59.94 on a Meetup.com organizer's subscription, created my own event, and posted that on the iPro event's page: "Anyone else who expected a meetup about Bitcoin and was sorely disappointed to learn the event had only a tangential relation? Have no fear. Join my real Bitcoin meetup. . . . Nobody will try to sell you anything."

An hour later, the account StyleWerxcom responded: Johnny and Bob and their outfit "came all the way from USA to share their crypto company with us and if your [sic] an investor you will know this is very valuable info to learn. USA companies work little differently [sic], and people need to have an open mind." I was banned, and my post removed. "No need for negative rants."

StyleWerxcom did not elaborate on the perceived cultural difference it cited, but its highlighting of the fact that the iPro people "came all the way from USA" amused me. Men from the south have long sought business in the northwest. Toward the end of the nineteenth century, American ranchhands came up to train cowboys. Fifty years later, when prospectors struck crude, southern oilmen taught locals how to extract it. But before all that — and not to cast any aspersion on my U.S. friends — one of the earliest American forays into the territory was the illegal whiskey trade, the exploitation of the Indigenous people's lack of alcohol exposure. One gallon of firewater fetched two buffalo robes. The herds thinned, and in the tall grass that grew in their place, men with revolvers and shotguns dealt dependency and disease — and death, for they resolved disagreements with the only tool they had. Cryptocurrency scammers are generally gentler, but they, too, peddle a sort of opiate, for at the base of their product is a hope and a dream, a respite from the dreariness of life.

I eventually found out that Stylewerx Communications was a marketing company by a cueball-looking man called Jan Cerato, listed on Meetup.com as the organizer of the iPro event and as one of the "Crypto Coaches" participants could "learn from." On Facebook, Johnny posted a picture showing Jan at the event, wearing bold white glasses and an equally bold button-down shirt with colorful paint sploshes. Johnny labeled Jan as one of iPro's "rising stars." I never did hear Jan speak that day, and he later wrote on his blog, *The Life and Times of JantheMan*, that he had nothing at all to do with the project and that the event itself was not actually organized by him. In the same post, Jan also wrote, without using a last name, an "Ethan," in his view, "went out of his way to slag me personally and create a MeetUp group specifically to out shine [sic] me."

I would find both those points untrue and baffling, if that "Ethan" was referring to me. I had been diplomatic when posting my event, doing so without casting any blame, without disparaging anyone or any product, but not only that — at the time, I had no idea who Jan Cerato even was, much less had any desire to "out shine" anyone. All I wanted was what I did not get at the iPro event at the Royal Hotel: to talk about Bitcoin and cryptocurrency with fellow enthusiasts.

CHAPTER 7

I arrived hungover to my meetup. The previous night, a reporter friend — who, months later, would serendipitously cover cryptocurrency for the Canadian Press news agency — had held a delightful end-of-fall party. I ended up an hour late to my own meetup, and every fiber of my being was cursing that I was even out of bed at all. "Why did I schedule the event at a bar?" I wondered as I walked in.

I was so late that one attendee already had to leave. It was Dave Bradley, who had been at the iPro event. He had a wedding to attend, Dave said.

I ordered a beer and a pretzel, both of which I touched sparingly. I mumbled apologies. There was a wide cast of characters, including someone who earnestly believed the Queen directly ruled Canada and had an active hand in governmental affairs, citing her face on money as proof.

The group that instantly drew me was made up of cryptocurrency "miners," the ones who run servers that facilitate transactions, generating new units for themselves at the same time. They form the backbones of most cryptocurrencies. Having legions of miners spread out across the world, each indiscriminately helping to process every transaction, is what keeps Bitcoin going without a central authority.

Two semi-bearded Venezuelan young men whose names I forgot — one tall, one short, like Bert and Ernie from the *Sesame Street* show — mined in secret in their home country. Mining is electricity-intensive and had become popular in Venezuela due to the negligible cost of power — "it's just a dollar," Bert said. Bitcoin had also become popular in Venezuela due to the country's collapsing economy and falling currency. Your grocery budget might afford 24 eggs one day, but weeks later, only twelve. There, a currency outside government control meant survival. But for the same reason — that Bitcoin was an attractive commodity in Venezuela — miners had also become prime targets of a government known for corruption. The government also did not like that miners were profiting off its energy subsidies. It cracked down heavily.

Winsor Hoang — an electrical engineer whose dark eyes perpetually glinted with business ideas, a trait he joked that his toddler had already inherited — had outfitted his basement for mining, with machines made from computer parts usually used for gaming. Michael, an electrician by training — who would later tell me, "I hold former titles from superintendent to 'asshole in the room' to project manager to 'the shark'" — had also turned his background to the power-intensive process of mining, setting up 30 machines in a house.

A month later, I chanced upon an online classified advertisement for mining machines for $600 a pop, less than half of the market price, and it was almost as if it were calling my name.

Those rigs were silvery rectangles roughly the size and weight of cats. They generated enough heat to steam up a room and the same amount of noise as a propeller plane flying overhead. People found ways to deal with that, for every unit was, as Michael described, a "money-printing machine."

The ad I saw was from a private seller, and the catch for the deal was that you had to pay up front and wait weeks for delivery. But everything was negotiable, I thought.

"I'll buy 100 if it's cash on delivery," I responded.

No dice came the response. "I can only do a prepayment option." The guy signed his encrypted email as "Jake." His username referenced the Soviet-originated auto brand Lada, described by *House of Cards'* fictional President Viktor Petrov as "the worst car ever built" and "a coffin on wheels." Jake's facility was in Russia, he said. Russia was banning mining, and Jake said he was looking to sell some machines and move the rest to Iceland — cold weather being good for the activity. I looked up the matter, and the news was reporting only that Russia was banning mining in apartments — hobbyist-type stuff, not the sort of scaled-up operation of a man who had at least 100 machines. But maybe something was coming, and Jake had some inside knowledge. "Nobody wants to go to jail" over $60,000, Jake assured me, and said he would be happy to sign an agreement beforehand. "By the way, you would have to pay lawyers' fees as well."

It didn't used to be that expensive. Mining rigs began as just everyday computers. But by design, the more computing power that goes into mining, called the "hash rate," the harder that process becomes, and so the more computing power is needed. Miners eventually had to use computers modified with multiple graphics processing units (GPUs), add-ons normally used for high-end video work or gaming. Still, they were often home-made. Then in 2013, Jihan Wu of Beijing — a financial analyst described by *Fortune* magazine as "strikingly reserved and gawky," who was the first to translate Satoshi Nakamoto's Bitcoin white paper into Chinese — founded Bitmain Technologies to make application-specific integrated circuits (ASICs, pronounced EH'-sicks) for mining. They were chips specifically designed to generate cryptocurrency and were magnitudes faster. Wu was not the first to have that idea, but his company would be known as the world's biggest. Machines that used ASICs, those with the size and weight of cats, soon replaced GPUs as the standard for Bitcoin. GPU rigs were still used to generate other coins, which was what Winsor Hoang from my meetup did. But even so, mining became more of an industrial, commercial activity, facing environmental impact criticism and increasingly out of the hands of hobbyists. Even as Russia targeted the activity, an aide of President Vladimir Putin would go on to own a mining firm.

I responded to Jake, "I'll need to think about it and talk it over with partners." I didn't have any business partners. But that wasn't a lie, I like to think. It was simply a statement that was not yet true. There was no way I would just hand that much money to a guy I didn't know, no matter how ironclad the paperwork. "Let me get back to you," I told Jake.

I reached out to Michael from my meetup, tracking him down on LinkedIn after losing his business card. I told him about Jake. "I know the saying that if something is too good to be true, it probably is." But it doesn't hurt to engage the guy, I reasoned. "Perhaps I can offer a higher price for cash on delivery, maybe I'll fly to Russia to escort the miners here, etc., etc. My main issue is that I don't have . . . liquidity." I did not want to risk that much of my own money. "If this guy turns out to be legit, I'm wondering if you are in any way open to sharing a lot of 100."

We never did go far with that deal. Jake backed out, for in his view policy looked like it was changing. "I am sorry, but we decided to keep those units for now. It's still not clear if the government of Russia allows us to keep mining. So, we'll see how it goes."

But Michael and I met up anyway, at the Palomino, a pub named after a type of pale horse. The place was too loud and too dark, and its interior design had too much wood, and the floor was slanted. The drinks were cheap, though. Michael said he would lend me a mining machine to get a feel for what the process was like.

It was the first time we had seen each other since my meetup. The talk got to the event with iPro. The man listed as the organizer, Jan Cerato, had started holding meetups that had nothing to do with iPro at a local gambling house called Cowboys Casino, I was told. Jan had not known what those guys from iPro were up to, Michael said. That was consistent with what Jan would publicly say. Later, the city's cryptocurrency pioneer Dave Bradley, who had spoken with Jan, told me: "He was very contrite when he came and talked to me, and he was like: 'You know, I didn't realize this was a scam. I see it now.'" The charge that iPro was in fact a scam, after all, had been unproven. Now Jan's new meetup was pretty good, Michael said. He encouraged me to go see for myself.

CHAPTER 8

Everything about Cowboys Casino was bright and tinted red, from the lights on the ceiling to the shine from the slot machines to the squiggly lines on the carpet to some of its neon letters outside, glowing like battered embers. The first thing that greeted me was the team of hired muscle in western shirts and black Stetson hats, the casino being a throwback to Calgary's early days, when it boomed as a cattle town. Gambling, whatever the sort, was often big business back then. The day the railway came to town in the late nineteenth century, and 400 local laborers got their salaries, a newspaperman estimated $5,000 changed hands in horse-racing bets before sundown. Perhaps those on the frontier had an inclination toward risk, for every one of them had already made one big bet with fate.

I had been at Cowboys before, back in 2014 during a brief trip to Calgary, right after Bitcoin had fallen 50 percent from my initial investment. I hadn't been to many gambling houses, so I didn't have a reference point, but Cowboys had felt like a very in-your-face casino, as if constantly screaming, "Me-gamble-money-sex!" I'd thought the tabletop dancing girls were a weird fixture. Nice to look at, sure, but I wouldn't pick this casino over another just because of their presence. Therefore, what quantifiable, tangible benefit did the women bring to the house? I remember thinking that and pounding back a few beers, and then losing every dollar I'd brought to the poker table. Despite seeing gambling in movies several times, I was still terrible at it. Maybe my despair that day unlocked dormant telepathic abilities and transmitted my thoughts to someone high up at the casino, for now, three years later, the dancing girls were nowhere in sight.

Jan Cerato held court in the casino's Japanese restaurant. He looked at home. Standing in front of his laptop, a screen behind him, he looked like a deejay. I would later come to see that he had a certain uniform: a baseball cap over brown hair shaved to the scalp, a black T-shirt, and glasses as white as his Apple AirPods earphones. There was a feeling of perpetuity about Jan, as if he had not simply been born a babe but had burst from the earth fully formed and then run straight to the casino. Jan was 46 years old but did not look it. He had that sort of agelessness that came with having no hair. I ordered salmon sushi and Sapporo beer.

As time went on, Jan would hold 100 of those meetups, roughly one every week. He called them "workshops," and there was a seminar-like structure to them. They happened mostly the same way, with Jan telling people about the great potential of cryptocurrency and blockchain. More than once, he talked about what he viewed as his vast experience in technology. "I've been on the internet since 1993," he said at one meetup. "I've watched internet every day. . . . I've watched YouTube and all these formats that we've come through. I've blasted through American formats and European formats that most of you've probably never seen." Jan did not elaborate on what those "formats" were, but he did say that the 25 years for which he said he'd "constantly studied media online" were 25 years "in a row."

Sometimes Jan would have local crypto-blockchain projects present at his meetups, and he often told attendees how they would still be considered early adopters if they got into Bitcoin then, that the whole journey from nascent to established industry hadn't even begun. "Going on a hike up a mountain — and we're still in the parking lot together deciding which way we're going." There were so many riches in that world. "I became an investor when I was 28 years old," Jan said. "Why I do this — it's all about the investing."

There were a good twenty people the night I went, a major improvement from the eight that turned up at Jan's first meetup. With Jan was his business partner Alex Jackson, a jacked, dreadlocked father of three, experienced in yellow-vested blue-collar work, a quiet man who rarely spoke at the meetups. Alex was Black, and Jan, a white man, thought the two were "like salt and pepper, and we're good together." On Facebook, he referred to the duo as "The white & black Panthers of #Bitcoin." Jan had pivoted to becoming, in his view, a guide for new entrants to cryptocurrency. He and Alex sold Bitcoin and offered private tutoring on everything crypto — services that Jan often promoted at the meetups. Their company was called Bitcoin Investments. Jan could move $5 million "within about" 48 hours, and under $1 million in 24 hours, he said. Jan felt his coaching had helped people make millions. "I have not helped anybody lose all of their money yet — thank God."

Jan was always entertaining when talking about cryptocurrency and blockchain. "It has got the Queen of England shaking in her shoes," he said more than once. Put a microphone in front of him, and you might as well be cranking the handle of a Gatling gun. At a later event, Jan would say he had been nervous for the first twenty meetups — "I used to get sweaty pits" — but the night I went, I never sensed any anxiety.

Jan certainly had a talent for public speaking and working a crowd. He was lucky that way, but luckier that, earlier on, he had found the perfect home for his gift. Jan had started a string of companies dealing with communications, branding, and construction. Jan's day job was as a marketer, running Stylewerx and the related Brandwerx. He seemed to have had some measure of success, being named a "notable young entrepreneur" by the lifestyle publication *Notable*. He believed he had established a good local reputation. "I have a trust economy that can't be broken," he said once. "My mom will tell you. So many people will tell you." By 2020, Jan wanted to be "in the Bahamas, spending half the year on a boat, docking at different beaches, and checking out exotic locations." He believed: "No, money does not equal happiness. Money is the ability to help create happiness and help people grow."

Beneath all of that, however, was a winding path. Jan had been evicted. He had racked up debts and had been successfully sued over them. He had been taken to court multiple times over his business dealings, although nothing had been definitively proven against him in those cases. He also had suspended charges for illegal confinement and assault. By all appearances, Jan was a man who, at one or more points, had been thoroughly pummeled by life. According to an assistant he hired late in 2017, Lannie Clarkson, a military-school alumna, Jan had told her that people "always underestimated me."

That would not be an uncommon profile for someone involved in the world of cryptocurrency. Bitcoin has a firm and well-known anti-establishment bent. Its earliest users were, after all, drug dealers and other exiles from mainstream society. The WikiLeaks whistleblower organization, for example, turned to Bitcoin to accept donations in 2011 after major payment platforms banned it. That underscored Bitcoin's potential to let users do whatever they wanted with their money, outside the control of any third party — an attractive prospect. In 2011, when Jan had racked up credit card debt of more than $12,000, the court ordered that, before he received his salary, part of it would be given to the bank. It is unclear how successfully that went, given that Jan ran his own business. But that sheer audacity of the establishment to just target Jan's wallet without permission? Such thinking would be highly ambitious with Bitcoin, which authorities had been able to seize only by exploiting human error. In 2021, a German prosecutor revealed that officials had tried to confiscate a hacker's cryptocurrency, but he refused to cooperate — and that was that.

When Jan showed up publicly in Calgary's cryptocurrency scene in 2017, it was as if he had become a new man. "I was so into cryptocurrency and Bitcoin, like, my mind was so here," Jan said at one meetup. "People at work would pull me aside — this week, in fact — and they said, 'Hey listen, you know, on Monday you need to come back to work, because you're too fucking crazy on your Bitcoin right now, you know?'" The audience laughed. It was funny because it was true. On his social media, "all you see is Bitcoin, Bitcoin, Bitcoin, Bitcoin, Bitcoin," Jan said. "It's like I have a problem. But how can I not, you know? Eight percent gain in the last 24 hours." Jan was Bitcoin everything. He would often wear a Bitcoin hat and a Bitcoin T-shirt, and his laptop bore cryptocurrency stickers. "If there was a cream, I'd probably put it on my face," he said at yet another meetup. "Sex and Bitcoin. Red Bull and vodka. They go together, right?" More laughter. "You can tell, already, from being here a few times . . . that I'm pretty passionate."

The night I was there, Dave Bradley came late to Jan's meetup. We greeted each other in the muted way people approaching in opposite directions might tip hats without breaking stride. Dave had become a regular attendee at Jan's meetups. After the iPro

Network event, from which Dave said he'd been kicked out, the two had developed a curious business relationship. Although Dave did not show much enthusiasm for being at the casino, he had the sort of impassive face that rarely betrayed enthusiasm for anything, and he forgave easily and was non-judgmental, holding firm frontier values of minding one's own business. Dave had become Jan's supplier. When Jan sold people Bitcoin, as Dave described, "he was buying coins from me and then reselling," taking a little off the top.

By the time the four-hour session was over, I did not gain any knowledge on crypto-blockchain that I did not already have. Neither did I exchange many words with Jan. But I left the casino never doubting that he was, in fact, a man worth getting to know.

I had no idea of the great personal tragedy that would result from my going to that meetup.

CHAPTER 9

I lost my bicycle.

At my day job at Reuters, I had always parked at the couriers' racks. You weren't supposed to leave bikes overnight there, but that had never been an issue. I rode the bike home every evening. Until one evening, in a last-minute decision, I decided to go somewhere after work far away enough that I had to take public transit. It was to that garish gambling house where Jan held his meetup. The next morning, my bike was gone.

I wasn't sure what to do. I'd never talked to building management. I didn't know who the relevant people were, in what crevice they lurked, or how to approach them. Maybe I'll just let it go. It wasn't even an expensive bike. In fact, it had been free. I had found it in my apartment building's smelly basement, thrown away by someone else. And plus, I had work to do.

But the matter stewed within me, and I started taking offence at that brazen thievery. How dare they take my hard-foraged bicycle? I turned up at the office that weekend to search for it. They — the proverbial "they," for I still had not the faintest idea who was responsible — must have kept it somewhere, for it was a good bike. It had dual suspension and ten speeds, and both brakes worked. What more can you ask from a bicycle? If

I'd had it longer, I was sure I would have named it and fed it candied apples.

It was the weekend before Halloween, and I entered the loading docks hastily that Saturday afternoon. I had a potluck to go to that night, and I did not have a lot of time. My bicycle was nowhere in sight, but in the great big electronic-waste bin that I would behold for the first time, I saw — stacked onto each other neatly, like black Tetris cubes — eight Dell Optiplex 780 computers. My God. Eight. They were missing their hard drives, but otherwise appeared to be in perfect condition.

With my earlier meetup and mining still fresh in my mind, I thought of using those computers to build GPU-based rigs that generated cryptocurrency. Specifically, I thought of Ether, the coin that ran on the Ethereum network founded by the team including Vitalik Buterin and Anthony Di Iorio. It was built to be resistant to the ASIC cat machines that were the standard in Bitcoin mining, so that everyday people could partake with homemade rigs. To Vitalik, the main co-founder, the dominance of ASICs, mostly made in the southern city that was China's technology capital, was no different from the centralization of power in, say, U.S. monetary policy — all it did was replace "eight white guys with a few dozen guys in Shenzhen."

I decided to haul home all the Dell Optiplexes and whipped out my phone to open the Car2Go vehicle-sharing app. The cheap blue-and-white two-seater Smart cars, which were the standard option and looked worse than Soviet Ladas, were not available. I had to go for the more expensive, luxury option and drove a Mercedes for the first time. For the life of me, I could not adjust the seat.

Building the rigs should not be hard, I thought. While I was new to mining, I understood the basics. And I've always been handy. My father's doctorate was in engineering, and he had involved me in home electrical work and taught me how to build a computer before my voice even broke. A young Ethan had taken great pride in knowing the family computer had a front-loading removable hard drive, and that we had two storage media for it, which could store a whopping 2.1 and 0.34 gigabytes. Whatever I did not know about mining, I was sure Google would fill in the gaps.

I carried each computer individually, first to the building's front door, then from the front door to the car. I would repeat that backbreaking process when I arrived at my apartment. It took 44 minutes, and the car cost $15.63. I decided I did not enjoy the Mercedes at all.

There was a coolness in the air, a chill that was more than autumn. I still needed to buy missing parts — the actual GPUs — and it would be weeks before the machines were actually put together. But that night — when I attended the Halloween potluck dressed as a policeman using a dollar-store toy kit, bringing twenty lukewarm Chicken McNuggets that turned out to be the star attraction of the night — thoughts of mining enveloped me like a fever. I was so excited, I'd forgotten about the bicycle.

CHAPTER 10

My one-bedroom Chinatown apartment was beside the Bow River, just a little up the waterway from where the Mountie Constable King had crossed, so named because the local Indigenous people had used the plants on its banks to make weapons to fire arrows. From my balcony, I could see the water rushing with energy, sparkling under the midday light, and a constant flow of people with it, either jogging on its sides or paddling through its midst. It glistened under the sun as if hemmed by silver, full of precious stones.

Inside, my apartment had become warm and toasty. I had the GPU rigs built from the Optiplexes and the ASIC borrowed from Michael, the electrician by training who had gone to my meetup, and for two months, I ran them 24/7. My apartment became so hot that, even in the last days of fall, I had to keep a window open to the balcony. I did not like that much as my balcony was caked in a thick layer of pigeon poop, beneath which was an absorbent, felt carpet that, in my mind, made it all worse. Yet even with the window open, I'd sleep without a blanket. In fact, I was shirtless all the time.

I had made a lot of money trading cryptocurrency, but found it to be backbreaking work, despite requiring no physical effort. It's like driving. You're sitting on your butt, but you have to stare ahead and pay attention. Every trading session felt like a workout. When I made a trade — my finger tapping the mouse as if about to squeeze a trigger — I felt the weight of all my ancestors upon me. After a while, when the novelty wore off, I stopped enjoying it. I don't think I'm cut out for that sort of work.

More and more, I gravitated toward mining. Working with my hands on my rigs gave me a sort of joy that staring at screens did not, even as I gradually gave in to the fact that my apartment had become unlivable. Aside from the heat, there was the noise. The GPUs did not make much, but the ASIC miner drove me crazy. I had a pull-up bar above my bedroom entrance, so the door could not be shut. Every time I closed my eyes at night, it was as if the noise somehow became louder. As well, even though I had electricity included in my rent, I knew nothing was truly free in this world. I lived in constant anticipation that my landlady would complain about the amount of electricity my machines were sucking up, which was probably enough to sustain a family of five.

I needed to move.

Winsor Hoang, whom I'd met at my meetup, needed to move, too. He had built mining rigs from 100 GPUs, and they consumed so much electricity, there was barely any left to run even a hair dryer. So Winsor and I teamed up. He and I went in on a dedicated facility together, a coffee warehouse with a marijuana-loving landlord. He needed the space, but none of the power. We needed the opposite. It was a perfect marriage.

No conversation about mining can, of course, escape the environmental criticism, that it is sucking up a lot of energy for no good reason. That issue is more nuanced and less clear-cut than it may appear. Those defending mining will say that even the premise of that criticism is unestablished — by what calculation or benchmark is the energy usage deemed a lot, and how is it purportedly for no good reason? But this is not the book for arguing that issue either way. Nor was I thinking about it at the time. Instead, I approached everything with a wild, reckless eagerness. Winsor and I quickly signed the documents and shook hands, and it was time for me to meet his family.

Winsor's house was in the northern part of the city, so north that it was north of the airport, probably touching the neighboring town, for all I know. It took me an hour to get there in a journey that included an Uber ride — an urban sprawl for which the city was particularly famous. Oil had thrust upon this young city a population boom it had never expected. Many say aldermen did not properly plan. Instead of building up, people erected houses farther and farther away.

It was only when I was standing in Winsor's basement that I could truly appreciate why he needed to move his operation. His 100 GPUs were so many that they needed their own room. The frames of the rigs Winsor had made himself from lumber. They were packed side by side onto Costco shelves. The machines reminded me of the 2000s rumor of the Iraqi government's purchase of 4,000 PlayStation 2 gaming consoles, using their combined computing to make sophisticated weaponry.

That day, Winsor's family and I had a lazy lunch of pho beef noodles, and then I helped the man on his Saturday project, building a ping-pong table. Winsor and I worked in his basement, just beside the room that held his GPU miners and their homemade frames. All the while, Winsor's rigs were making him money that amounted to more than $3,000 per month, and that figure was growing.

Of course, everyone else's digital gold was piling, too. After I left Winsor's house, I checked prices, and Bitcoin was up 7 percent for the day. I had begun the day dipping tendons and meatballs in a mixture of seafood dip and hot sauce with Winsor, then washing them down with Moosehead beer, from the same east coast city of the newspaper at which I'd interned years earlier, and then I played with spanners and screwdrivers, and I ended the day 7 percent richer. But later, looking back, I would realize, in the grand scheme of things, that 7 percent was nothing.

CHAPTER 11

Toward the end of 2017, Bitcoin was approaching its peak at the time of $20,000 apiece. It would touch that price only briefly and on certain indexes, but even without hitting that exalted round figure, the rally still made many gloriously rich. The Winklevoss twins, the same brothers who'd famously fought Mark Zuckerberg over the Facebook social network, became the world's first publicly identified and undisputed Bitcoin billionaires. (Estimations of Anthony Di Iorio's net worth ranged between $750 million and $1 billion.) Media coverage and Google searches were on a similar crescendo as Bitcoin's value, so much so that it had become unclear whether price sparked attention or attention price. Traditional investment firms increasingly started offering products based on Bitcoin. Mainstream interest shone white and hot.

My Reuters colleague Nia, a Welshwoman who knew as much about Bitcoin as I did the moon, and who had no idea of my involvement with cryptocurrency, brought up the subject out of the blue. Nia peeked through the gap in the computer screens that separated us to ask, "Ethan, do you have any Bitcoin?"

"Oh boy!" I thought. "This is my moment." Nia was not prepared for my ensuing speech.

"What a fascinating person Ethan is," I like to think she thought.

But I didn't tell Nia the whole story. There was one piece of information I omitted, for I'm a very private person. For example, I once tried unsuccessfully to list my job title simply as "employee" on a credit card application. I've also tried, also unsuccessfully, to display only my last name on another credit card (to be fair, the application had a "preferred name" field, leading me to believe going by one name was possible). I've delisted my birthday on Facebook, and if I could, I would hack into the government database to redact that from my birth certificate as well.

I didn't tell Nia how rich Bitcoin had made me. Up to now, I haven't told anyone, not even my own parents. Even when directly asked about that, I have always deflected. I realize the irony of saying this publicly now: I was a millionaire.

Even though I was the one person who knew that little nugget of data, I did not grasp it well. In a way, it was a sort of news even to myself. The run-up to what was then Bitcoin's all-time high had been swift and sudden. The rally from $10,000 to $20,000 would happen over roughly two weeks. Relative to the event's impact, that was an infinitesimally small window, barely enough time to take a spit. Moreover, in terms of prices, the entire period had been turbulent and seesaw-like, making one live in the moment rather than be pensive and analytical. I knew vaguely that my fortunes had risen, but I had not had the chance to consciously process the implication until Nia asked. As I sat in that outpost of an office in Reuters orange and gray — where the cubicle walls blocked the heater to make the room icy cold, but where the midday sun reflected off neighboring buildings, forming a beam strong enough to kill several ants — I suddenly realized, if I so fancied, I could pick up the phone and buy an elephant. If I were older, I could retire and drink in the day and use seasons as verbs ("I've always loved the south of France, but it's so full of upjumped new money lately; where do *you* usually winter?"). Squeezing that modest idea into my head filled me with a certain satisfaction, like the first gulp of tea in the morning, hot and spreading not just through the chest but also into the empty belly.

The surprise at my unexpected good fortune, I got over that quickly. Luck is not random, I've always believed. The Romans had a goddess of luck, Fortuna. Whether the toga-wearers actually believed in a woman living in the sky, the fact that they'd distilled a faceless elemental force into a sentient being says something about how they viewed luck — the philosopher Plutarch had an entire speech about how fortune favored Rome, having caused the rise of its empire. Emperors built temples and put Fortuna's face on coins. Generals took her as their patron. The Romans also plainly laid out a more direct method for influencing Fortuna — "Fortune favors the bold" was their saying. And depending on your definition of bold, research after research has proven that truism true: people who consider themselves lucky are simply those that look out for opportunities and are unafraid to try new things. I clearly did not cause Bitcoin to rise toward $20,000 or predict that rally in any way, but I believed there was nothing unearned or undeserved about my new riches.

I felt a surefooted stillness, as if I had grown taller, my chest broader, and my shoulders more swaggery. The next day could bring civil war or locusts, and the skies could rain blood, and I wouldn't care. It was as if some sort of wolf within had suddenly made itself known.

Then, almost instantly, I wanted more — and there was indeed more. Cryptocurrency had only been around since 2009. Everything was still in its infancy. Like everyone else I'd met, I had been seduced by this new world and its potential and opportunities. Later, when searching for a simple explanation for what I did next, I would cite this, that in that moment when I came to truly understand my wealth, my heart had been filled and pierced with bewitchment and with desire, for the enchanted gold beyond price and count.

But really, it had been seeded for years. Research has shown that our brains subconsciously make decisions before we realize it. Our subsequent, rational decision-making process — we think we objectively weigh pros and cons, but perhaps we are merely justifying to ourselves a commitment already made. My poking around on the dark web, my pessimism at my generation's financial outlook, my initial purchase of Bitcoin, my first faint idea to write this book, my disquiet in my job, my restlessness in my life, and my lust for novelty and tolerance of risk — everything about me had been building toward that day.

That day, after I talked with my colleague Nia, I thought, until my thoughts were as knives. I started typing up a farewell email: "I was an early adopter of Bitcoin and will be running my cryptocurrency mining operation full-time." In the subject line, I referenced my favorite television show at the time, which was adapted from a book series. I quoted a character dead and then resurrected, who leaves an organization he joined only because he knew no other path, and who has gained a new, more personal mission, even though he has little idea where it will take him: "My watch is ended."

ACT III

2018 HIGH: $17,700

CHAPTER 12

There was one last piece of business before I left Reuters. High noon, I arrived at a redbrick and blue-glass downtown block to meet the team of Oleum, a startup that combined cryptocurrency and oil and gas. That ten-story cube it was in, almost as wide as it was tall, was known informally as the Field Law building, named after its main tenant, a storied legal firm more than a hundred years old. Formed after the death of illegal whiskey and the gold rush, after the Mountie fort was formally incorporated into a municipality, and after the railway had come to the land, Field Law came of age in the ruins of the Old West, growing together with its city amid the cattle and then the oil boom. That building into which I stepped — with "FIELD LAW" in giant, but also classy and understated, silver letters on its side — was the marker of a new era, of rebirth.

Over lunch in Oleum's conference room, I got to know Steve Carter and his team. Steve was described as having "over fifteen years of management and entrepreneurship in various industries including security, transportation, and the service industry." A goateed man with an eye for money, carrying some slight bulk, Steve had invested in American real estate in the 2008 financial crisis and started a luxury-lifestyle service before founding Oleum. With him was Dave O'Connor, Oleum's co-founder and a frequent collaborator, who said he was an old oil-and-gas hand, a graying man, friendly but not overly so. The team had just returned from an Ethereum conference in the Mexican city of Cancun, at which Vitalik Buterin had spoken. There was a third Oleum co-founder, and he did the most talking. I fancy myself good with faces and a bit of a detective, so as soon as half the food was gone, I realized he was Dave Bradley from my meetup. He brought the cryptocurrency muscle.

Oleum was the perfect melding of two worlds for a city like Calgary, Alberta, the sort that thrives and lives and dies by the boom and bust. The city's fate was so intrinsically tied to the unpredictable price of oil that, in 2015, it changed its slogan to "Be Part of the Energy," from the previous "Heart of the New West." This boomtown understood at a visceral level what beat within cryptocurrency, even before Satoshi Nakamoto and the Genesis Block. It was, after all, a vigor it had long known, yet had not seen in a long time.

The year 2017 was a particularly low point for the Alberta oil industry, with the withdrawals of major internationals including Shell, which took with them a more than $20 billion footprint that would have translated into jobs and tax revenue. It was the continuation of a long-running decline, and its effects were everywhere. My personal theory was that it was even responsible for the coldness I felt that day on the seventh floor, despite the overwhelmingly yellow lights and the easygoing lumber design that lined the bottoms of the white walls: office thermostats had been calibrated to account for the heat human bodies give off, and nobody thought to turn them up when layoffs and bankruptcies emptied downtown. I didn't know if that was actually true, but it seemed logical. After all, when conversation turned to livelihood — and sometimes even lives, for the local suicide rate rose with unemployment — it would not be surprising if building management deemed everything else irrelevant. "One of the first budgets they cut is the art," Verne Busby, who made two fancy paintings for Oleum's lobby, told me later, recalling how he had to contend with lower rates for corporate clients. Thus those 0.7 square miles in the center of town were left drab and frigid — all the misery of the West.

But the opposite was happening in cryptocurrency and blockchain. That new world had reached peak euphoria. "ICO [initial coin offering] financing was just going insane this year," the Oleum co-founder Dave Bradley told me. By the end of 2017, projects would have raised $5 billion in total. Their ICOs were not even all held on Ethereum, for rival platforms had emerged. Even celebrity endorsements were entering the fray, including from the actor Jamie Foxx, boxer Floyd Mayweather, socialite Paris Hilton, rapper The Game and music producer DJ Khaled, and, of course, the noted warrior-thespian Steven Seagal. Before he died, the broadcaster Larry King had sat on a blockchain company's advisory board. Celebrity endorsements ran so rife that the U.S. Securities and Exchange Commission issued a warning: just because the people pushing a product are famous, it does not mean they "have sufficient expertise to ensure that the investment is appropriate."

The market had become wall-to-wall crowded with coins. There were technical distinctions between an ICO token issued on a platform like Ethereum and a coin that had its own block-chain, like its native Ether — or Bitcoin — but they made little practical difference to the investor. It was all just cryptocurrency, and by then, there were more than 1,000 different coins. Some of the new coins, the altcoins, were made for specific reasons: to bring perceived functional improvements, such as privacy, for example, or to serve as a medium of exchange on a partic-ular platform, like Ether on Ethereum. But some had less clear purposes or value prepositions, even if they were not malicious scams. There were so many coins based on marijuana alone that publications were creating top-five lists. One, Potcoin, rose 60 percent after it sponsored the American former basketballer Dennis Rodman's self-described peace mission to North Korea, a country that, incidentally and separately, seemed to have developed its own fascination with cryptocurrency — a fascination that fascinated me as well. Some altcoins appeared to be little more than jokes, like the one called Coinye West, after the controversial hip-hop artist, or Dogecoin, based on a shiba inu dog from a meme. Both had preceded the ICO boom, but in 2017, while Coinye had already been practically killed by a Kanye who did not appreciate the humor, Dogecoin surged more than fifteenfold. Investors had become so hungry, you could create a coin for almost anything.

So why not a coin for North American oil? Oleum combined digital and black gold, selling coins to raise money for oil companies hit hard by the downturn. The Oleum tokens would allow investors to claim royalties when those companies drilled. The idea was essentially a collaboration of the Daves — Bradley from cryptocurrency and O'Connor from oil. It'd also once involved another oilman not present, with whom the company had fallen out and pushed on without: Dale Galbraith, who looked to be in his fifties, built thickly but in a dynamic way, with a tooth or two knocked out from hockey, fading white hair, and a past in politics that the mayor had once described as being part of a "backroom." Dale was a sort of good ol' boy of the city whose role had been to provide corporate support — both in terms of money and access to lawyers and oil connections — in exchange for a minority stake.

But it had all begun with Steve. "Steve kind of put two and two together," Dave Bradley said. Steve seemed to have a knack for that, like how he sensed his real-estate investment opportunity in 2008. In cryptocurrency, there was a ghost of the bygone days, when the boomtown was a land of dreams. Mathematician, engineer, truck driver, or even high-school dropout — there was a six-figure oil-patch job available if you would but spit in your hand and shake someone else's. You, too, could afford flashy trucks to haul your all-terrain vehicles, just like all your neighbors. In a city like mine, the Oleum team could easily get investment with which to begin, and there was no shortage of distressed oil companies that would want funding through the project.

Oleum listed ten oil companies as committed partners. In the new year, Oleum was going to list its coin on the Dutch Caribbean Securities Exchange, which had developed a special platform for such issuances, Dave Bradley said. Many of those smaller countries in the Caribbean and Europe — traditionally tax havens with permissive policies — had seized onto the crypto-blockchain boom for the investment dollar. "We were shocked at how good it was," Dave said of the Dutch Caribbean exchange's platform. "It really is an amazing step forward."

The day we met, Steve looked every bit like his picture on Oleum's website, in which his tie was a little off-center but his suit slick, his hair styled, and his goatee trimmed. In front of the wood-panel background, Steve looked like one of those downtown office workers with single-syllable names like Brad or Chad, who wear gray Patagonia fleece vests over pastel Armani shirts and schedule their lives around when the financial markets open and close. Steve was looking to raise $200 million through Oleum's token sale, and he looked capable of such a feat. The sandwiches and pizza we ate that day, after all, were not the fast-food, cheap kind. They were the artisanal kind that cost twice as much for half the portion. There was a difference between the two, and as I tasted it that day in the Field Law building — Verne Busby art of flatland and sky hanging in the lobby below — I instantly thought Oleum was serious business and that Steve was a serious businessman.

It was true that Steve did not have a background even remotely related to the field, but that was unnecessary. In crypto-blockchain, nobody cared about who you were before, because there was no before. It was no law society. There was no test to pass the blockchain bar. Everyone involved in the field was new in some way, even the most wizened and the cleverest. It's like that little town beyond the territorial border, where new houses and gold claims pop up every sundown, where you get paid by the day, and where nobody asks your name. Steve's story was not just his own. It was also mine, and mine his, and ours everybody's.

CHAPTER 13

Inglewood sits east of downtown, but in the nineteenth century, it had been the downtown. It was Calgary's first district, sitting where two rivers meet, where the Elbow flows into the Bow. A little west of Inglewood, just across the Elbow, was the Mountie fort of pine and spruce that had spawned the settlement, built with timber that had been chopped upriver. The district had been developed by the government gunmen themselves, and boasted the settlement's first "main street," the early sign of cityhood carved out of the wild. Now it was a hipster slice of town.

In Inglewood near the train tracks — between graying telephone poles and their wires, in a two-story squarish house, with brown walls, a red front panel, and a white top — lived the bald, bespectacled, self-described "Crypto Wealth Coach" Jan Cerato. The house doubled as his office, and skateboard decks lined the walls inside, shiny and unused, along with a guitar and a bicycle. Beneath the skateboards was a lit sign showing a stylized Bitcoin *B*, bright and orange and big as the coffee table on which it sat. The house was where Jan held his private Bitcoin workshops, and strings of people constantly came and went. It would become a sort of chrysalis. "As Bitcoin and blockchain knowledge was assimilated by Jan, his mind could again see new avenues to develop," according to a profile of the man in a cryptocurrency magazine he founded, riddled with typos and formatting inconsistencies. Parts of the year had gone by in a blur for Jan, and now he had a whole five-year plan. "His reach and influence," the magazine profile on Jan read, "inspired him to start another company named Blockchain Wealth Capital, which focused on using blockchain technology to help fund and develop businesses new to the industry." Jan would later say the project was not his idea.

It was, however, an opportune time for such an idea. In 2017, the Coinbase exchange, founded in San Francisco, became cryptocurrency's first proverbial "unicorn," valued at more than $1 billion. Crypto-blockchain was attracting mainstream investors more so than ever before. But many lacked the will to learn what a Bitcoin wallet was, how to get money onto an exchange platform, or how to safely store the resulting coins — all the nitty-gritty details that early adopters had internalized over the years that made all the difference between profiting and losing everything. And if you worked for an institutional investor like a bank or hedge fund, even if you'd learned all that, good luck explaining it to your boss, who fondly remembered the days he wore a bright blue blazer over suspenders and shouted buy orders on a crowded trading floor, cigarette in hand. Mainstream investors wanted to just tell their brokers to buy Bitcoin or something and get it done. So crypto flooded the wider investment market. Doing anything blockchain meant big bucks, for there was intense FOMO (fear of missing out) on the part of investors, a worry that a lack of action might lead to permanent loss, thus making participation necessary and urgent, like love in wartime. Famously, New York state's Long Island Iced Tea, which made sweet drinks, changed its name to Long Blockchain and saw its shares more than triple in value. A headline for a *Wired* article about attracting investment read "Is Your Startup Stalled? Pivot to Blockchain."

Then there was the reverse takeover. Cryptocurrency companies, flush with cash, were buying existing publicly traded ones and then changing their names as an easy way to list on the stock exchanges. The new world was pushing outward, puffed with potential, pulsing and pounding like some gigantic heart. The shares of a Vancouver gold miner surged threefold the day it was born anew as Hive Blockchain Technologies, which mined Bitcoin. That listing method was exactly what Blockchain Wealth Capital was going to pursue.

Playing a lead role as president and co-founder was Jan's childhood friend Scott Fleurie, who once headed a listed company, a banker serious enough to have been mentioned several times in the country's fancy newspaper of record the *Globe and Mail*. He was the kind of guy who knows big finance words like "backwardation" and "fiduciary," and his name had appeared on those boring press releases with long disclaimers about "forward-looking statements." In a different sort of press release, one prepared for "the first publicly traded full regulated Investment Bank of Crypto Currencies in Canada Called Blockchain Wealth Capital," Scott said, "When I saw what Jan was doing I knew I needed to get involved."

"Scotty," as he was sometimes called, was "the most legit guy" of the team, according to another member, Dani Noriega, a self-taught trader with curly hair originally from Guatemala. Dani was to handle the cryptocurrency markets. The head of research was to be Kirk Matthews, sometimes known as "Captain," likely thanks to a certain science-fiction television series. In his non-cryptocurrency life, he was an engineering consultant. Alex Jackson, Jan's business partner, was to be head of sales.

Through the bitter solstice that marked the shortest day of the year and the chest-fluttering rally that sent Bitcoin to $20,000, Scott labored over Blockchain Wealth Capital presentation slides for more than 48 hours, making at least 72 revisions, meta-data from the file showed. In a group chat on Telegram — a Russian-founded encrypted-messaging app favored by privacy-loving cryptocurrency enthusiasts, which eventually went into the sector itself — Scott hounded the team for biographies and headshots, telling them he wasn't asking twice, even though he did: "I'm meeting with the President of the Venture stock exchange Friday and I want this presentation wrapped up. Im not asking again." The venture exchange was a kind of little brother to the Toronto Stock Exchange, with lower listing requirements. Long dependent on natural resource stocks, it had been quiet due to that sector's downturn until industries such as blockchain heralded a revival. Vancouver's Hive Bitcoin miner, for example, traded on the Venture.

"Ok, I'll get that to you asap," Dani said, the only one to respond to Scott.

When Scott reported back, he did not mention any president but said a meeting with two lawyers had gone well. "Let's just say they like the idea so much, they aren't even charging us for their time and want to be part of it! We are going to be on the exchange 100 percent." Almost a week later, Scott had "3 great meetings": "I actually have people hunting me down that want to proactively work for us including a high profile CFO [chief financial officer]." Scott said in the Telegram chat, "I believe we will have bankers fighting for this deal, money is not a problem, I am dt [downtown] today meeting with some more bankers and also meeting . . . to discuss office space, exciting times guys." Scott had wanted to raise some $2 million. Another week later, he said, "Bankers loved the presentation, they are having a conference call with Vancouver group this afternoon to discuss."

"I knew they Would!!" Jan responded. "You killed it, im super proud of You." The same day, Jan posted Scott's slides on

Facebook, saying: "Our new company Blockchain Wealth Capital Corp is going to be a stock on the TSX. Were [sic] buying up a bunch of Blockchain & Crypto tech firms from Vancouver, Toronto & Montreal. We will be the biggest Blockchain Corp in Canada History!! Get Involved Early!!" At the same time, a new advisor to the project was considering coming onboard: Elias Ahonen, a Finnish-Canadian political-science graduate who had started the blockchain company Token Valley, which had been hired to help consult on Steve Carter's Oleum.

Two weeks after he publicized Scott's slides, Jan posted a screenshot of Blockchain Wealth Capital's website, saying, "Ladies & Gentleman we are officially Live!!" The sleek page, with a black background and white words on a bluish globe, read: "The revolution will not be televised. It's happening now. On the blockchain."

Then the website went down.

The following is extracted from a press release by Jan Cerato. It has been selectively excerpted for length, but is otherwise unedited. It is unclear if it was ever sent, and Jan would later say Blockchain Wealth Capital was not his idea.

Bitcoin Investments

For Immediate Release
Contact: Jan Cerato

Back in September Jan and Alex began hosting a meetup for friends in Jans living room, shortly after the group got too big. They decided to taking it out on the town. Since then Jan and Alex have done 23 meetups and have grown a following of over 800 people on meetup.

Outside of the meetups Jan and his team offer one on one Coaching sessions. Group coaching sessions, at home mining rigs, Investment opportunities and a plethora of other opportunities for anyone to get involved in Crypto.

One of the most exciting is the first publicly traded full regulated Investment Bank of Crypto Currencies in Canada Called Blockchain Wealth Capital. Scott Fleurie the President and CEO of Blockchain Wealth Capital was childhood friends with Jan.

" When I saw what Jan was doing I knew I needed to get involved." Scott Fleurie

" Bitcoin Investments and Blockchain Wealth Capital, have the same fundamental backbone, which is to help the community gain accelerated wealth strategies through Crypto currencies" Jan Cerato

CHAPTER 14

Jan's father had died in 2012, and in December 2017, as Blockchain Wealth Capital took shape, his mother had a stroke. Jan pleaded with Jesus to "ask our father to look after my Mom" and to "please keep her alive in the hospital." Jan would sometimes talk cryptocurrency with his mother. A chart of the 100 largest Bitcoin holdings, billions upon billions, "made my mom, you know, eat her socks," he said at a meetup. The news of the stroke was the last thing anyone needed. It did not help that Jan had anxiety. For years, he had taken pills that muted his emotions before switching to marijuana. It was a gray Christmas, the harsh snow, both in the air and on the ground, made just a shade darker by the ashen sky.

Then despite all of Scott's hard work on Blockchain Wealth Capital, the financier told me later, "after two months of setting up the company, I received a call from the ASC [Alberta Securities Commission] with their concerns — due to crypto being unregulated." Canada does not have a federal regulator for listed companies. The local commission in every territory holds paramount power. Scott declined to elaborate, and it is unclear what exact concerns the regulator had or how the call came about. But that call would not have been surprising. Ever since the collapse of Japan's Mt. Gox, ever since 2013's high-profile takedown of the illicit dark web marketplace Silk Road, authorities across the globe had been watching this new world with keen interest. With the entrance of mainstream investment into crypto-blockchain, that interest had intensified, particularly from the bodies that usually regulate finance.

The commission was no joke. Once, I ran into its director of enforcement, Cynthia Campbell, at a conference. I made no introduction beyond my first name, and I doubt she remembered it, but she struck me deeply as someone very serious. "For those who wonder," Campbell said at the conference, "uh, should I just take my chances and see if I get caught?" — she proceeded to recount how a staffer once uncovered industry wrongdoing without knowing that the target had already self-reported to others at the commission. "We're out there," Campbell said. "We're actively looking." A commission lawyer would tell me six enforcement staff had worked in cryptocurrency. So when the regulator called, Scott paid attention. "I stepped away at that point," he said. "I was never paid or received any money from this venture, just a lot of wasted time." Separately, the Oleum consultant Elias Ahonen told me he had declined to participate in the project. The major law and finance firms named on Blockchain Wealth Capital presentation slides told me they had nothing to do with it. The company was never "going to be a stock," as Jan had described.

J an disliked heavy regulation. In a question-and-answer section of Jan's magazine, when asked, "Do you fear any sources of regulation affecting your business or use of crypto?" he responded, "I feel it is necessary to some degree. But . . . people should be able to vote on the rules and regulations. . . . The people will be able to apply the best strategy and principles of regulation, rather then selfless [sic] organizations!" At one of his meetups, he described the concept of governmental enforcement in ICO fundraising as "regulation bullshit talk" that was "some sort of block in the freedom of it all." Jan added, "Half of me, as a person inside Bitcoin, agrees with protecting the people, and the other half of me disagrees with the control that brings."

Jan, however, was not one to wallow or to get beaten down by life. In fact, he was the opposite. There was a constant energy that coursed through Jan. According to his profile in his magazine:

> Some have said that men cannot multitask. Anyone who has made these statements has not ever met Jan Cerato. Back in high school, he was given the nickname "Janspeed" because he was always buzzing with enthusiasm. He frequently was doing more than one thing at a time and most people had a hard time keeping up with him.

Aside from everything Bitcoin that Jan was already doing, he also wanted to organize conferences in different cities, sell Janspeed "performance" cryptocurrency mining machines, and start his own exchange platform, calling it "BitSpeed." "I'm an entrepreneur, and so was everyone around me," he said at one meetup, talking about the local cryptocurrency scene. "We had a million ideas, you guys — we had a million ideas right down to, like, Bitcoin underwear, okay. It was crazy what we thought of. Right? Like seriously, I know it's funny, but we thought of things." What would become the most prominent project associated with Jan was what he called a "whaleclub" pooled investment service.

Whales are wealthy casino patrons who get special attention because they spend so much. In cryptocurrency, the term refers to people who hold large amounts. The whaleclub would have people hand over money or Bitcoin to traders who would actively play the market. The service would take its cut from the profits. How the project was structured, whose idea it was, or even who was officially in charge would later become the subject of much dispute. What is certain, though, is that what the whaleclub did — play the markets and trade cryptocurrency — was at least half of the mandate of Blockchain Wealth Capital. The same people — Jan, Scott, Dani, Kirk, and Alex — worked on both the whaleclub and Blockchain Wealth Capital, and they talked about both projects in the same Telegram group chat. While Jan would later maintain he was not in charge, he promoted the project, dealt directly with investors, distributed their money to his whaleclub team to trade, and frequently issued instructions in the Telegram chat. "Ok guys we have new funds and a new plan to start fresh on monday," Jan told the team on January 5, 2018, a Friday. A day later, Jan, who had said he had a five-year plan in cryptocurrency, promoted the whaleclub on a wider, public-facing Telegram group: "Im here to make this club wealthy, I've committed to all of you for 60 months of my life." Jan continued, "I will personally help every single good honest person in our club."

Monday, however, would reveal itself like cigarette butts under the snowmelt.

In Jan's Inglewood house, the crew was seated around a table. Jan was in the big chair in the corner, his usual space beneath the skateboards. Outside, the sun peeked through broken clouds as a gentle wind blew north. The fact that it was the beginning of the traditional workweek had little significance. It might as well have been a Friday, for that was the day after the markets had hit an all-time high. By then, the more than 1,000 cryptocurrencies had appreciated so much, their combined value was more than $820 billion, nearly hitting the magical thirteen digits that would thrust the new asset class into the same trillion-dollar club as gold or oil. It was the realization of whispers from nineteenth-century California. Gold swam in streams like carp and bristlemouths. Grab a pan, bend your back over the waters, and rise a baron. The whaleclub people had traded through the weekend.

Among them, Dani Noriega called himself the best trader, which had indeed been his reputation, and his trading logs show he knew what he was doing. It was not a high bar, for none of the whaleclub people had a deep background in the matter. Self-taught, Dani was just a faster learner, and with the cryptocurrency rally, he told me, "This was like the easiest bull market to trade." But that day, the profit he had made was the last thing on his mind. Sitting around the table, Dani was nervous. He had been preparing for a speech. He was going to say what the men older and more experienced than him might not like. But Dani needed to say his piece. After Jan had finished talking, Dani, who had questioned the legality of such an investment club, told everyone he was out.

"Have you spoken to a lawyer?" Dani asked. "Have you spoken with anybody about legitimizing this project?" Whatever the jurisdiction, to offer investment products to others comes with a lot of paperwork, rules, and disclosure requirements, a heavy regulatory burden meant to protect investors. "I spoke with somebody, and I basically determined that I needed to get out of this."

According to Dani, Jan said, "Okay, like, I'll send you your cut, you know."

"I don't want anything. . . . I think things will go badly," Dani replied. "I don't want to be anywhere close to this."

Dani might as well have spontaneously combusted. Jan was certainly not expecting it. While Jan did not address the incident when I brought it up to him later, the fact that Dani left that day has been corroborated by two others who were in the house. I also heard about the matter from someone who helped put Dani in touch with the lawyer to whom he'd spoken. With Dani's resignation, the temperature of the room changed, he told me. "They kind of looked at me not very favorably."

As Dani left the house that day, he said Jan told him, "Don't worry about anything. I'm going to talk to some lawyers, we're going to get straightened up legally, and you'll have nothing to worry about."

That gave Dani a little hope, even if he did not fully believe it. "Talk to me when you actually talk to a lawyer, because I'm not gonna hold my breath," he thought. But even so, there was a joy rumbling within as he walked out into the crisp air hovering around zero, cold yet unusually warm for that time of year. "I knew I was doing the right thing, and that's all I could ask."

Later that night, Jan posted a copy of the securities laws on the Telegram group, saying, "We are good as far as the legal confines of these rules right now!

"we cant take any fake ass management fees

"Only brokerage fees

"we are not breaking the law or securities laws so far :)

"and i had no plans too either, for the record!

"i had my aunty who is a paralegal get me the docs and read the rules for me."

In the same Japanese restaurant in the red-tinted casino where he held his meetups, Jan gathered a group of more than 40 people for what he called his "private Bitcoin Investments club."

Jan wrote on Instagram, "I'm excited to turn you all into profitable Crypto Investors!" Some time later, he wrote on Facebook: "Crypto Investors Whaleclub filling up Fast! Get your funds in by Friday, to take advantage of the Gains in this 90day window! Don't sleep we take cash, cheque, bitcoin, ether & alt coins similar value. Pooltime! msg me or call for details." Jan's Facebook profile was somewhat public, with posts visible to those who were not friends.

"How fast did they double their accounts?" someone commented on Jan's post.

"Ninety days max," Jan responded. "Some did it in less than a week." In response to someone else, he repeated the claim, "We double in 90 days max."

"Five days for me," Scott said.

I would learn of these activities only much later, when I set out to write this book and started interviewing the people involved. At the time, despite how interesting I found him, I barely knew Jan and paid little attention to him. We had only a brushing, tangential connection, that of two people from different worlds. Still, Jan tried to directly recruit me into the whaleclub, sending a flyer that said the team was "ready to trade for a group of investors who are interested in growing their crypto currency and don't have the time or experience to play the crypto markets. Msg me if you have the $10k to play." The flyer featured a Ferrari F50, a twenty-year-old speedster of which only 349 were made, which fetched as much as $3 million on the second-hand market, red as the décor of the casino where Jan held his meetups. The term "Lambo," a reference to the Italian sports car brand, is a meme on the cryptocurrency internet, alluding to explosions in wealth. But the Ferrari on the whaleclub flyer appeared seemingly without context. Was it to suggest whaleclub investors would be so rich that they could buy it? It was curious, to say the least. I did a reverse image search online and found no matches, indicating the picture had not been simply grabbed from the internet: it was an original. Did Jan take it? Or — was it his car? Was it to show that the guy running the operation was successful and should be trusted? Whatever the case, increasingly, Jan sure lived like the sort of man who would drive that car.

CHAPTER 15

As the Lunar New Year celebrated in Asia approached, Jan invited the crew to his house for the 34th birthday of his girlfriend, Angie Coombes. Jan also sent a wider invitation to his Facebook friends, but there, he made no mention of Angie's birthday. "Happy Chinese New Year!!" he wrote. "Big Party at my House tonite 7-11pm!! If you luvv Me come through and Visit." Angie's birthday had somewhat coincided with the Asian holiday, and while Jan was part Italian, part Polish, and white as a fish belly, he had long had a taste for Asian culture. Moreover, 2018's festivities were significant for Jan because it was the year of the dog, the Chinese zodiac symbol under which he was born 48 years earlier. It was "my sign and my year," he said on Telegram.

The party of ten included Jan's cryptocurrency associates Scott Fleurie and Alex Jackson. The Oleum contractor Elias Ahonen was there, too. There was also Jan's assistant, Lannie Clarkson, a redhead who liked wearing bright yellow. Before cryptocurrency, she had worked as a chef, and she remembered vividly the food at Jan's gathering: "Sweet-and-sour chicken, ginger beef, fried rice, garlic-steamed broccoli." Hard liquor and soft drinks flowed. Colorful strobe lights bounced on shiny skateboard decks on the wall. It was a boisterous night, for Jan's girlfriend, Angie, was a musician of local renown. Wearing a white, stringy, and form-fitting jumpsuit full of holes, she played the keyboard in the kitchen and sang an original composition, "Falling After All." Sitting on Jan's sofa next to the bright orange Bitcoin sign, she strummed her guitar and led the party on a wild drinking song about a Russian pub, "Kretchma," performed with an exaggerated eastern European accent. Multi-instrumented, genre-bending, Angie was no doubt talented and was the sort that livened up any party. But if you were a guest that night, you would be excused if you said your highlight had nothing to do with the birthday girl. That night, Jan did something far more memorable. "He wanted to, like, show a token of his appreciation," said his assistant, Lannie.

Before the night began, Jan had called his gathering a "Big Party" and said, "let's Blow it Up bigtime together!!" And he did not disappoint. Above a glass table and to the left of the skateboards hung a screen that showed a screensaver-like video of different cities. During the party, Jan had people guess the names of those places and would then hand winners some $100 each as a prize. They also played Cards Against Humanity, and Jan gave the same amount to those who attained milestones in the party game, often arbitrarily defined. "It was pretty clear he just wanted to give everyone $100, and that was how he went about it," Elias said.

Financially, Jan appeared to have been doing really, really well, and he — who supported the Children's Wish Foundation and the Heart and Stroke Foundation and, in 2015, donated to an organization offering children's summer camps — was a man fond of paying it forward. I never found out exactly how much the whaleclub was managing, but it was definitely a lot. Statements sent to investors pegged it at around $200,000. Alex put it at double that. Jan himself told Elias, in a conversation about whaleclub investors, "They trusted me with a million bucks, and they trust me even with more." Jan had become a notable figure on the local cryptocurrency scene and, for many, was the primary destination for everything Bitcoin. "They trust me, and they love me," Jan said of investors. He would also sell more than $1 million worth of Bitcoin that he had sourced from the early cryptocurrency adopter Dave Bradley. Life was good, sweet as a slushie.

Three weeks after Jan's Chinese New Year gathering, one week before the Ides of March, he and I happened to be at the same party at Elias's apartment, just steps away from mine in Chinatown, close to the river. It was around midnight, and the party had gotten wild to the extent that all half dozen of the guests had tried dancing on the living-room stripper pole, whose presence in Elias's apartment would take too long to explain. But my interaction with Jan was brief. I still hadn't paid much attention to him, and I was leaving as he arrived. Jan and I exchanged few words beyond the usual greetings. The city was empty and frozen as I walked into the night.

At the time, I had continued to hold my own meetups, for no other reason than the fact that I had already bought a Meetup.com organizer's subscription. I made sure to hold the events on different days from Jan's, although the entire matter wasn't something to which I'd given much thought. There was no structure to my events, and I had no services to promote. All we did was talk about cryptocurrency over beer. Most of the time, it was the same handful of people attending, and I didn't care if they came or not. Jan Gregory Cerato, on the other hand, who had promoted services at his meetups, had a fundamentally different philosophy about organizing them. Later he would write in a blog post that his events at the casino "had taken off like wildfire, every Thursday night was getting busier and busier, the word on the street had gotten out all across western Canada that Jan Gregory was the new Crypto expert and 1000's of people came."

After I left the apartment, Elias and Jan left as well to get wontons, and the former summed up their conversation to me: "He kind of told me: 'For me, this is all a business, you know? Everything I do is business.'"

Outside, a midday ice fog had cleared, and a slow wind pushed southward. On the banks of the Bow, a gust stirred in the cottonwoods, and the melting snow swelled the river that rushed black into the night. The frost was mixed with the mud, dull under the starglow, as if marked by faint cigarette stains.

Much later, Jan told me in a text message: "i dont take it as serious as most do. I dont care about it like you think i do. Im using the crypto movement to my advantage . . . to capitalize on the moments." At one cryptocurrency meetup, he said: "What's the focus? Making bacon." And he smacked a palm face-up upon another, as if the paramount importance of money was as simple and obvious as the color of grass. "Right? Like, that's all it's about."

For all Jan's talk of passion in cryptocurrency, he also remembered hardship, as he wrote on Facebook: "There were times I had just $10 worth of gas in my tank. . . . I've had just $50 to feed myself and my family." No one can be blamed for seeing the new world of cryptocurrency only in tangible, transactional terms, as if a homesteader yawping at the black bubbles of an oil seepage, heart heady with desire for a life that had been elusive. Who wouldn't do the same? Even among thinkers and artists, there's none completely unmoved by material gain. There's a bit of a Roman in every Greek. While I do not like to admit it, the truth is, I would find that I was little different.

CHAPTER 16

My farewell email at Reuters was a hit. "Ethan, that is a killer send-off," responded Morgan, an Australian who almost two years earlier had taught me how to use the company's internal software while mocking my taste for BlackBerry phones. "You are clearly destined for great things."

I wasn't even the only one with such a story. The company's former general manager for the Americas, Saul Hudson, a different person from the famed musician of the same legal name, reached out to me: "I hear, like me, you have jumped from Reuters to blockchain. It would be great to share notes."

Almost immediately, my old employer interviewed me for television news. Bitcoin had fallen a little, but it was still strong at $15,000 per unit. Like the swarms of pundits crowding the realm, I said in the interview that Bitcoin would at least double its price by the end of 2018. The city asked me for cryptocurrency advice. I spoke at local meetups. I appeared in all sorts of media. A particularly enjoyable experience was when I wrote a long piece about myself and cryptocurrency mining in a fancy magazine, the *Walrus*, which was a bit like Canada's *New Yorker*. To write again, to immerse readers in worlds they'd never see, to introduce them to people they'd never know, and to add unnecessary literary flourishes my editor would hate, and then go over the word limit — I felt alive. As the single-named Trevanian writes in *Incident at Twenty-Mile*, "Some trades leave their marks on a man, like those little burn-scars on the arms of a blacksmith, or the black spit of a coal miner."

At the same time, I thoroughly embraced the more radical changes to my life. They would happen, and had happened, over a long period, but in my memory, it was just one big blur. I reached out to a real estate contact — Curtis, whom I'd met at my first meetup and to whom I later sold several thousand dollars' worth of Bitcoin — to ask about buying a house. My business partner, Winsor Hoang, and I hired our first employee. So much money was pouring into the cryptocurrency sector. I attended business meetings at snooty private clubs. I would have breakfast in Vancouver and then dinner in Hong Kong. I went to Washington for one day just to attend a party at an embassy. I caught a flight for no reason other than to see the Toronto Symphony Orchestra play the score of the first Lord of the Rings movie as the film screened, a performance as glorious and majestic as it was unnecessary. I was at all sorts of Bitcoin conferences whose organizers were flush with new wealth, filled with open bars and the finest food at the fanciest hotels, and full of the most interesting people. I swear I was at one point eye to eye with broadcaster Larry King as he said of Bitcoin, "I have a feeling it's all going to be very big."

Even my parents saw that — firsthand. The cryptocurrency I'd given them years earlier as Christmas presents had risen so much in value, I had to google how to describe the appreciation in the Latin-prefix way of double, triple, quadruple, et cetera — it is "vigintuple," although I'm not sure if it's an actual word. That surge in value was enough for my parents to see things my way, to see what I saw in that new world. It was not an earth-shattering development, to be sure. For me, I no longer cared for any parental validation. It had gotten to the point that the only way I measured myself was the value of my cryptocurrency holdings. For my parents, the windfall wasn't a lot: $40 simply became $800. They did not have the energy to deal with a sum in Bitcoin that small, so they just gave the haul back to me. But all of that felt good nonetheless. Everything was adorable and easy, cool and crispy like a fresh apple.

So it wasn't long before some guy from Russia hacked me.

That's not unheard of. While the Bitcoin network itself has generally been considered impregnable, granting users absolute control over their assets means there's no recourse if someone improperly obtains your private key, the equivalent of a password. A common saying goes, "Not your keys, not your coins." Exchange platforms, such as Japan's Mt. Gox, have long been targets, having lost a collective $15.6 billion toward the end of 2019, according to one estimate. With the surge in prices in 2017, Bitcoiners themselves increasingly came into the crosshairs. Summits became prime targets because so many cryptocurrency holders were all in one spot, so much so that Bitcoin.com published the article "How to Survive a Blockchain Conference without Getting Hacked." In Austria, a man lost €100,000 in Bitcoin after he logged on to a public WiFi network. All over the world, an unlucky few were even detained and tortured to hand over their coins. The financial-crime lawyer Christine Duhaime, who once represented Gerald Cotten's QuadrigaCX, would write that murders and violent robberies of cryptocurrency executives were up 100 percent in the first half of 2018 alone. At one Toronto conference, I saw the Ethereum co-founder Anthony Di Iorio now had bodyguards. I also know of a far more interesting story on that subject from another crypto big shot that I've promised not to repeat.

For me, I had woken up to find in my inbox a login alert for my email account — from Russia. Then I saw login alerts for my cryptocurrency trading accounts in my inbox. Using information found in my emails, the hacker had tried to access those accounts to withdraw the funds. I could feel my fingers tremble on the keyboard.

But then, as I assessed the situation and tried to figure out my next move, I saw I had lost no money. I had two-factor authentication for my cryptocurrency accounts. You needed more than my login credentials to access them. I stupidly had not had that for my email, hence how the hacker was able to gain access. The contents of my messages were probably worth a fair bit as well, but to exploit them would require a lot of reading and operational finesse, and the hacker had not gone to the trouble. That led me to believe it was a mass attack, and that I had not been specifically targeted. Amid the tide of relief, I changed all my passwords, and the incident then became a funny story I would tell friends.

Much later, I was on a Thai island partying with members of a cryptocurrency incubator — which gave funding and early support for startups, in exchange for a stake in the business — housed in a hillside resort. Elias Ahonen, the Oleum contractor, was there with me as well. At the end of a hard night, I lounged by the penis-shaped pool whose structure had taken me a whole week to notice. During the incubator's crazier days, people used to have orgies in the water, I was told. The big boss who funded everything was an early Bitcoiner and had made a fortune, but he had little experience — or perhaps even the will or desire — to run an incubator. People had come and gone, staying for free, indulging in unchecked merrymaking. At least once, they had allegedly brought over a shaman. The "burn rate," what was needed to maintain the facilities alone, was $20,000 per month. Elias, a world-traveling-adventurer type of guy, later returned to the island and would tell me even crazier tales involving a convicted murderer and local mafia, but that is a whole other story.

On the rocky isle, I sat where the cliffs met the wild wind and watched the rising sun pick out the textures of the unyielding mountains in the distance, losing their blackness against a brightening sky. They looked not that different from the foothills of the western prairies, which began life as ancient seabeds. Sometimes when you hike them, the saying goes, you can see corals and other remnants of the deep. Now they touched the sky.

There was some sort of a business purpose to the trip when it began. I had planned to write off my costs as a company expense. Then I changed my mind when I could not point to a single business matter that arose from that trip. The longer I stayed there, the longer I had no idea what I was doing on that island. But there I was, somehow content that I had the ability to not care. It was as if I was scratching an itch I never knew I had, and it was glorious.

The locals had just had their first election since the Thai military overthrew the civilian government in 2014. At issue was the rule of law and democracy, yet underneath ran the same bread-and-butter concerns everywhere: half of Thai millennials were in debt and one in five had already defaulted, and they were less likely to own property than their parents. Meanwhile, the over-60 population was set to double by 2050 — an increasing tax burden. As young Thais forged and found their place in the world, a pressure bore down on their shoulders the size of the Spanish-American War. My friends and I learned about the Thai election only because, on polling day, nobody would sell us booze.

That morning as I lay poolside, the remnants of Ecstasy, speed, mushrooms, and LSD coursed through my system as I welcomed the dawn, the morning glow red and molten at the bottom. We were high up and on an island, and the sapphire sky was unmarred by anything unnatural, wider than the eye could see. If you told me I was looking at the entire sky of the hemisphere, in my altered state, I would have believed it. It was a Verne Busby painting. It was nature's IMAX. The clouds, pink and then mauve, were as ships, sailing from one corner of my vision to the other. I saw ravens, sleek and slender, swirling in the stratosphere and men in canoes paddling the Technicolor streams below, which I was pretty sure were only in my head. In that moment, all I could think about was when I last sat and saw a sunrise. I could not recall. I was not on the island long, just a little more than a week, and I didn't do anything impactive or challenging, but even if all memories of it fade, I will never forget how, for a few fleeting moments that day, the world looked like perfection.

CHAPTER 17

Back in my city, I received a lunch invitation from Oleum. "This event will be catered by Spolumbo's, so bring your appetite," it read. I was instantly sold and asked no questions. I had no idea what Oleum's "Bitcoin Rodeo Supporters Lunch" was for.

Anybody who was anyone in the local cryptocurrency scene was invited to the Oleum office that day to break bread with the co-founders, Steve Carter and the Daves Bradley and O'Connor. Government people. Bank people. Startup folks. Elias Ahonen. Lannie Clarkson. There were about twenty people, and the room was packed so tightly I couldn't get a seat at the table. Jan Cerato, who arrived later than me, had to stand. It was a "meeting of the chiefs," with "new things brewing," as Jan described the event. Even with all the people, the building still felt cold, and I thought my previous theory on the temperature was rubbish.

It turned out we were all going to be asked to sell tickets. Oleum had been organizing a conference called the Bitcoin Rodeo. There was little talk of selling coins to fund oil companies that day. It was just the rodeo. Dave Bradley wanted to bring in a show pony. It was then that I recalled Dave had told me about it earlier in an email that had quickly slipped my mind. "We've set up a ticket sales referral program for a few people we think might be able to help us sell tickets," he had written. I would earn 15 percent of any ticket I sold.

As Bitcoin rallied, just like how you could slap "blockchain" onto any company name to make its stock soar, you could slap the same onto a conference name and watch the dollars roll in. Sponsorships, ticket sales, you name it. Bitcoin had fallen by early 2018, dipping below $10,000, but it was still more than four times higher than its price from six months earlier. The market widely believed it was on the way back up. The Consensus event in New York, by the news outlet CoinDesk, was considered the world's biggest, and in 2018, it brought in an estimated haul of at least $8 million. "It's crazy," an organizer for another conference, who was familiar with the San Francisco scene, told CNBC. "In the Bay Area alone, there's a conference every week."

At the head of the table with Dave Bradley, Steve Carter held a Dasani water bottle as he chaired the meeting, elbows off the lacquered table like a man of fine breeding. He wore a navy suit jacket and a light blue tie finely patterned, complete with cuff links on his white shirt. Steve wore Apple AirPods, indicating he was the sort of busy man who constantly expected to receive phone calls, but needed his hands free for other activities because he was a busy man, and also did not have the time to take off and put on the earbuds because of how busy he was. Oleum standee banners, one black and one white, stood behind Steve, flanking the company president like flags. He listened intently as others spoke, his goatee fresh, clearly shaven recently.

Almost an hour into the meeting, from the back, I heard Jan say, "I'll give $100 in Bitcoin to everyone right now!"

Heads turned, and all eyes were on Jan.

Dave was in his black T-shirt, doing the whole work-uniform routine favored by chief executives and world leaders, like Mark Zuckerberg or Barack Obama, in which they wear the same clothes every day to cut out unimportant decisions. But almost all the other people were in office wear. They surveyed the man in the slogan T-shirt and baseball cap, perhaps as they would modern art they didn't understand. Then the room went back to their conversation — "Have we considered the margin of error on these projections?" or something boring like that, to which someone would respond, "Yes, quite." But afterward, people swarmed Jan like hungry children. At one point, he had to add a caveat: he would give Bitcoin only to people who did not have cryptocurrency yet. I asked whether he would give some to my sister in another city, and he said no.

In my memory, Jan gave Bitcoin to at least five people. I can't remember what exactly Jan exclaimed after each transaction, and it seems neither can any others. Their recollections include "Yahoo!" "Booyah!" and "Woohoo!" No two people seem to have heard the same word. But there is no question Jan shouted to express excitement each time he gave away Bitcoin, as he raised a fist into the air amid all the eyes upon him. I should not have been surprised. Despite — or perhaps because of — his past struggles with anxiety, he was a man who constantly posted on social media the virtues of inner strength — "nothing stops my self esteem [sic] from overcoming everything!" read one Twitter post, tagged "#persoanal [sic]." The doling of the Bitcoin alms that day was like a Renaissance painting. If I could travel back to any moment in history to witness anything, the Baptism of the Uninitiated and Feeding of the Multitude by Jan "the Man" Cerato would be in the top ten, easily, along with, perhaps, the Battle of Thermopylae.

I don't profess to know what goes on in the mind of Jan Cerato, but I like to think I understood the display that day. I myself had started talks with my alma mater to set up a scholarship. It was fancier, of course, but fundamentally it was no different from what Jan did. It wasn't about generosity or a desire to flaunt wealth as much as it was out of restlessness. On Twitter, I'd offered one bitcoin to any reporter who would publicly and seriously ask U.S. President Donald Trump about his country's relations with the comic-book African state of Wakanda, after a comedy writer's offer of $300 went viral. (Anticlimactically, nobody took either offer.) As much as I traveled, which I did a fair bit even before Bitcoin, I hadn't made any tangible lifestyle upgrades. I eventually decided against buying a house as I did not think I would remain in the city for long. Once so coveted, real estate now seemed like a ball and chain. I didn't buy a boat or a car. I was fed with the same food, used the same electronics. I still whipped out a calculator application at the grocery store to get the most grams per dollar for cheese. When you suddenly have more than you usually use, you don't quite know what to do with all the money.

I thought about that as I watched Jan instruct the line of first-timers to download a wallet app — Jaxx, created by Anthony Di Iorio, incidentally — to receive his Bitcoin. I continued pondering as I walked out of the meeting that day, past Verne Busby's paintings in the lobby. Maybe I would buy art, I thought as I took a closer look at Verne's creations. They showed a hazy infinity of flat prairie green and middling mountains that rolled and billowed like a tossed blanket. The rocky ridges stood agelessly against a silky sky and gargantuan globs of sleepless clouds, white and angry like the river rapids. Verne's work depicted "profoundly moving chaotic forces," he had said. The paintings captured two different snapshots in the timeline of a storm. One was called *Turning towards Calmness*, the other, *Moments Before*. I was in awe, although to my untrained eyes, the two looked the same.

It wasn't long after thinking that thought that, like everyone else with a lot of money and no real job, like the American former basketballer Dennis Rodman, I decided to go to North Korea.

INTERMISSION

NORTH KOREA

CHAPTER 18

While I grew up in Germany, I was born in northeastern China, whose porous border let in thousands of North Korean defectors. Higher in the hierarchy, some of the country's elite studied at my parents' alma mater. I've heard stories of how those students had the sort of arrogance born from being untouchable — a reputation not that different from some of their Chinese counterparts, which is expected, for I've also heard that the China of the mid-twentieth century was not too different from the North Korea of the 21st. I've long been curious about closed-off, totalitarian states, places of less opportunity. Both my parents had ended up as engineers, and I've always thought it was more than passion that set them on that path, particularly for my father, a literature buff and the one person I know who can read classical Chinese. I've always wondered if I had been born and bred in a place like North Korea, would I have turned out differently? When the country announced a blockchain conference, I knew I had to go.

It's not easy to go to North Korea, one of the most reclusive and restrictive places in the world, but it's also not impossible. For the blockchain conference, there was an application process, and then the forking over of €3,300, the bulk in cash upon arrival and €800 of it prepaid. The methods for prepayment:

no credit cards, no easy remittances to the great Bank of North Korea, only a wire to some obscure financial institution in Estonia or a transfer of Ethereum's Ether. I chose the latter because it was less painful, and luckily for North Korea, Ether rose by as much as 50 percent in the ensuing two months, resulting in a 50 percent profit from simply doing nothing. All of that perfectly illustrates the curious link between North Korea and cryptocurrency, which critics say threatens global stability, a connection built entirely on what that dictatorship is and its place in the world.

After paying the €800, I picked up my visa from the North Korean embassy in Beijing and had a Peking duck dinner with fellow attendees, none of whom I had met before.

The first thing one said to me was "What made you decide to risk your life to go to North Korea?"

"Well, what about *you*?"

We all laughed.

"We all share a certain sort of crazy," I said.

The next day, we flew to Pyongyang on Air Koryo, once the world's only one-star airline (out of five) and the only one on which I'd flown that did not board passengers by zones. While Koryo did in fact have a business class, there were no classes at the gate, where everyone boarded together. But the door was only so big — normal door-size. Not everyone could board at once, so there was still a queue. Whoever got to the gate quickly was still first, and the laggard was still last. That was funny because everything else about the airline also evoked the Cold War. Koryo's entire fleet was at one point banned by the European Union because its Soviet-era planes had safety issues. They even looked retro. And the flight attendants still wore the high heels that many other airlines had retired over sexism and form-over-function concerns. In their uniforms, they were all thin and tall and dolled up in such a homogeneous way, it was clear they were chosen for their looks. Perhaps the country wanted shock and awe, to bust stereotypes. The first thing a friend, a bit of a social media influencer, asked me about North Korea was if the women wore makeup and heels. She was surprised by the answer.

Formed after the Second World War, North Korea has never played well with most of the world, pursuing nuclear weapons against the West-led order and being accused of rampant human-rights violations and criminal behavior. So the world hits North Korea with economic sanctions, which in the postwar decades have become the favored fist for showing displeasure. In the increasingly intricate webs of international trade, only a handful of currencies are widely used, granting power to their issuers, for controlling a currency also means controlling the infrastructure used to move it. The United States, with the most transacted currency, is often the prime mover in many collective sanction efforts, locking target countries out of international trade. In the two years of 2016 and 2017, the United Nations sanctioned North Korea more times than in the previous twenty.

Enter cryptocurrency, which can be moved without central-ized control and whose transactions can be difficult to trace. Theoretically, if used correctly and with the right infrastructure and resources behind it, it could help North Korea overcome sanc-tions. Since 2017, observers have increasingly said the country was amassing cryptocurrency. North Korea allegedly hacked exchange platforms in South Korea, operated large-scale mining efforts, and deployed ransomware attacks that demanded payment in digital coins. By 2019, the country's government hackers had hauled in more than half a billion dollars in cryptocurrency, according to a United Nations report. Any North Korean interest in cryptocurrency would also be at least partly ideological.

The idealized independence that cryptocurrency grants, after all, is reflected in the country's state doctrine, Juche, which preaches standing alone and depending on no one — the incompatibility of cryptocurrency ethos and the country's broader communism ideology notwithstanding. In 2017, an article on the website of the government-controlled Kim Il-sung University, named after the leader Kim Jong-un's grandfather, stated that in order to improve the country's financial structure, it was vital to master cryptocurrency. Experts believed Kim Jong-un himself had given a thumbs-up to the conference. The organizers said there had been huge interest. There is thus a formlessness to cryptocurrency. It grants freedom from the financial system. It represents a new structure immune to the whims of powerful nations. But whether that is good or bad is often a matter of perspective.

Of course, all that information I'd known at the time about North Korea and cryptocurrency had been observed from the outside. Much of what we think we know about the dictatorship comes from defectors and Japanese and South Korean intelligence, each with their own agendas. As well, lots of viral North Korean news can be traced back to unreliable sources. Kim Jong-un's ex-girlfriend had been reportedly executed. She later turned up on television, alive. International media once picked up a story of how Kim's uncle was executed using 120 wild dogs — dramatic but ultimately proven false. What truly was happening on the ground in North Korea with respect to cryptocurrency? Some experts said the conference's purpose was to send a message to the United States and its allies: that North Korea could defeat sanctions using cryptocurrency. Analysts and law enforcement were expected to be paying keen attention to the event. It was a golden opportunity to see for myself what North Korea had been up to. I ended up, by all measures of that word, surprised.

Maybe I should not have been. There is much about North Korea that you can never read in books or watch in the news, much you can never understand from afar. With North Korea, while you may never know what you will get, it will always be unexpected. That was a realization seeded before the blockchain conference even began — many times, in fact. Once was when I observed the trials of a fellow attendee, the guy who had asked me why I wanted to go to North Korea, who sat next to me on the plane and who started taking pictures of the Barbie-like flight attendants and North Korean passengers in boxy suits with Kim Il-sung and Kim Jong-il pins. A flight attendant approached him and insisted he delete the pictures and show her that he did so. Then when we landed in Pyongyang, the man had his laptop taken away for images of his ex-girlfriend the local authorities construed as porn. The North Koreans promised to give it back when we left, and they kept their word. But it had been a dark and foreboding event, as if an omen. In that moment, at the culmination of a plan months in the making — the sum of much anxiety, excitement, effort, and cost, and a cold Air Koryo chicken sandwich famous for its terribleness to cap it all off — a knowledge rumbled within me, clearer than ever before, that I had stepped into a different world.

CHAPTER 19

'd thought the blockchain conference was big, but the day before we flew from Beijing, at the Peking duck dinner, I found out I was one of only eight foreigners going. At first, I'd thought there were going to be other attendees not present at the dinner, but it turned out that it was just us. On arrival, I discovered the conference agenda had yet to be determined. The next day, two days before the actual summit, to my surprise, the attendees were asked to be presenters. While at least one among the eight was already supposed to be a speaker, most did not expect that. As the group's only person with the relevant skin color, I was asked to present on the preapproved topic of blockchain in Asia. I declined.

I had been particularly jittery about the trip. Journalists were explicitly barred from the conference, and thus I had neglected to mention my media experience in my application for the event. It was no misrepresentation, to be sure, for I was not employed by any organization, and I was on no specific reporting assignment. And I did tell everyone all of that after I'd landed in North Korea, and nobody seemed to care. But before that, I had been overthinking that and many other things. I had taken to North Korea a blank computer that contained nothing but one season of the Netflix show *Russian Doll*, which I never ended up watching, and a burner phone. I was also mindful of the geopolitical sensitivities, of how hot button the issue could be of giving or even being seen as giving technological aid to North Korea. I was there as a conference goer. No way was I going to present.

For that same reason, I will not be saying too much about who my fellow attendees were. I name only those who have publicly said they have gone: Christopher Emms, the organizer, a Brit with a background in finance, good at karaoke but bad at using chopsticks; the Italian information-security specialist Fabio Pietrosanti; and an American living in Singapore, Virgil Griffith, who worked for the Ethereum Foundation, the main force behind the eponymous blockchain platform. The rest were mostly assorted Europeans, the youngest of whom was my age. We had little in common other than the fact that we were all in North Korea, but that was enough, and we knew that. We happy few. That spring of 2019, beneath portraits of two dead Kims, we sat through an improvised two days of halting blockchain presentations.

In China, there's a rent-a-white-person industry of sorts. It's been declining, but it exists, especially in lower-tier, less international cities. The Caucasian would usually be paid a couple of hundred bucks, given some important-sounding title, like "director," and asked to give a speech or attend a fancy dinner, although some gigs are more creative. In 2017, a car-repair shop wrote an ad looking for white Westerners to "perform as mechanics." The idea is that a white face conveys an international image. Property developers, for example, want to show their backwater towns as globalized cities. A white face also adds prestige. Having one makes a company seem connected and successful. The actual background of the hired foreigner does not matter. "Audiences are watching you for your skin color, not for what you are doing," the American director David Borenstein, who made a documentary on the phenomenon, told the *South China Morning Post*. "It's kind of like being a monkey in a zoo." I felt my group's presence at the North Korean blockchain conference was a little like that, too.

The Koreans called us a "delegation," to be trotted to the center of the conference room and address about 50 locals. They gawked and laughed at three foreigners — including Ethereum's Virgil Griffith, whose Alabama twang, if you listen closely, still lurks somewhere in his way of speech — who, on the second day, showed up in freshly tailored Mao-style suits with the Mandarin collar. We slept and dined in their finest places, but we had no idea who the conference audience was, were given no one-on-one contact with any attendees, and they probably had no idea who we were, beyond what we said we were. We seemed to be just token foreigners.

There was nothing new discussed at the conference, no information presented that could not be found on page one of a Google search. The presentation materials, which had to be preapproved by the Koreans, were just publicly available research papers. I never got to hear from a single North Korean about the country's alleged work or plans with respect to cryptocurrency, and I was disappointed at that.

The thing is, though, our North Korean minders said the country did not know anything about cryptocurrency or blockchain, and there was definitely some truth to that. Even the name of the event had to be changed to "International Conference on Finance" because the organizers on the North Korean side deemed "blockchain" too alien. I talked to a waitress, and she did not know even the term "Bitcoin." It wasn't just that she did not understand the inner workings. She had never heard the word at all. I could not even explain to her why I was in her country.

In a meeting with one of the country's biggest corporations — and I have no idea why that was arranged — a senior executive told me the little unspectacular blockchain tinkering of his organization was the most advanced in the country. Wondering about the reports I'd read, I asked the company man what North Korea had done in cryptocurrency mining. He told me there was nothing. The country did not even have enough electricity for domestic consumption, he said, which was definitely not a lie. The actual blockchain conference was only two days, but we had a whole week in North Korea. In the days before the conference, our minders had brought us to a teachers' college, and while we were there, the power went out. It also went out several times at my hotel, which was supposed to be Pyongyang's best.

The image of North Korea that I'd gleaned from the widely circulated reports — using cryptocurrency to evade sanctions, hacking millions from exchange platforms, and generating new units through the electricity-intensive process of mining — was nowhere in sight. At one class at the teachers' college, the instructor used an unactivated version of Windows, and domestic businesses we visited flaunted at length completely unspectacular technology like television media boxes, 3-D movies so boring I fell asleep, and arcade games that seemed to be decades old. One of them involved shooting cows, and that was about it. There were no objectives, no levels, no challenges in the game. I can't remember if there was even an end — you just grabbed a gun and killed animals in unending carnage.

We think of North Korea as stuck in time, yet constantly perpetuating great evil. But if you'd have seen what I had, you'd find that Western view of North Korea — backward yet sinister — to be quite contradictory. It's hard to believe the country is capable of anything at all. But I do not doubt I was shown only a small, curated part of it. I have no plans to be a public-relations guy for North Korea, saying all is well. In fact, a running theme of that trip was the subjectivity of truth that has been a hallmark of Cold War–era totalitarian states. In that dictatorship, people believe the United States started the Korean War, and that their side "won" it. Objective facts are a rare commodity. Perhaps it had all been an act, just as how the foreigners at the conference were putting on a hastily cobbled show of blockchain for them. Performance within performance. Yet there were some things that I'm sure were not theater.

The North Korean women were afraid, for someone had pulled the snake from the bottle. I hadn't seen who had done it, but out in the open, the dead serpent was. The bottle was empty. We had drunk all the snake wine. Sixty percent alcohol. It's particularly healthy for men, our Korean minders said earlier, sniggering. Sitting in that karaoke lounge — dark and smoky, where three nights earlier, Virgil Griffith impressed us with his rendition of R.E.M.'s "Losing My Religion" — my head was spinning. I could make out that a Mandarin-speaking foreigner, newly met at the hotel, was extoling the virtues of buying a North Korean bank, but that was about it. That was my last clear memory, talking to that Mandarin speaker with the big face and big hands. I didn't quite feel like myself again until the next night, when I ran into that guy again, and he bought my party fine wine totaling €400 and talked about his bank plan yet again.

I never really learned anything in North Korea, except for the sharp taste of snake wine, which was itself an experience, and the hospitality of our hosts — we got along with them so well, we hugged when we left. Many nights were like the snake-wine night, some sort of unexpected drunken revelry. Each seemed to blur into another with its sameness.

What I did perceive, however, was a constant reminder of the geopolitical tensions all around. The Mandarin speaker had wanted to use my name to get a loan to buy a bank. At least, that's what I could remember and make out. I never speak good Mandarin when drunk. That proposal sounded shady in every way. It was a signal of the dangers of dealing with North Korea. The sanctions loomed large over our trip, just like everything else to do with the country, for it had been a sensitive time. A tragedy was still fresh in the memory. Otto Warmbier, an American who had been detained in North Korea, had died upon his return home due to what his parents said was torture. With worsening tensions, insults like "dotard" and "rocket man" had entered the diplomatic lexicon. U.S. President Donald Trump held two unprecedented summits with the North Korean leader Kim Jong-un, all sound and splendor, signifying nothing, but they were high profile and thrust the issue firmly into the zeitgeist.

The day after the snake-wine night, as we woke still reeling, not far away, also in Pyongyang, the leader Kim boarded a train for Russia, toward Vladivostok and Vladimir Putin. The leaders had a gala and shared a toast, and exchanged gifts of ceremonial swords, and then President Putin publicly backed Kim's position in talks with the United States. And one day, as I walked out of an elevator, I ran into a Chinese military officer, for whom a flock of Mercedes sedans — supposedly barred for export to North Korea — waited outside the building.

"That's a three-star general," I said, half a statement, half a question.

"Yes," my North Korean minder said, with a smile. That was the highest rank in the People's Liberation Army.

Aside from the literal, there was also the figurative China I observed. A university professor might speak accented English, but even service staff spoke pitch-perfect Mandarin. Chinese electronics and Chinese cars — the shadow of North Korea's uneasy Elder Brother ally was everywhere. Like in the Korean War that began in 1950, the peninsula was not just a battleground in itself but also a proxy arena for struggles between bigger powers. It was a powder keg. Analysts feared a nuclear crisis.

Against that backdrop, it would not be surprising if cryptocurrency and blockchain, issues already mysterious and with a sometimes unsavory reputation, would be deemed extra evil if associated with North Korea. Even as some locals were literally falling asleep during the conference, half a world away, there were those who sat up and paid attention. None of us knew then how focused that attention was.

By the time of that trip, it had been a year since Jan Cerato had given away cryptocurrency at the meeting for Oleum's Bitcoin Rodeo conference in Calgary. I had become older, more haggard, but only wiser in terms of what I knew and could envision. It was overcast on the last night of the North Korean blockchain summit. As we drank €200 Chinese *baijiu* to mark the conclusion, readying ourselves to return to real life, the stars overhead were cloaked against the black Pyongyang sky, and nobody expected that something stirred in the West — a sleepless eye and peerless resources. Trouble brewed in more ways than we could imagine or foresee, and it would compound what we had all already gone through in the cryptocurrency world over the previous year.

Presented verbatim:

Program for the delegation

18ᵗʰ April
17:10 Arrival at Pyongyang Airport
18:30 Check-in (Potongang Hotel)
19:30 Discussing the program

19ᵗʰ April
09:30 the Grand People's Study House
10:30 the Museum of the Victory in the Korean Liberation War
14:30 Pyongyang teacher training colleage
16:00 Mokran-Kwangmyong company

20ᵗʰ April
09:00 **Kim Il Sung** Square
10:30 the Tower of Juche Idea
11:00 the Arch of Triumph
11.40 Wolhyang Exhibition
14.30 Pyongyang Bowling Centre
15.30 Maeari Indoor-shooting Centre
16.30 Korean Stamp Museum
17.20 Handicraft Exhibition

21ˢᵗ April
08.00 Departure for Kaesong
10.30 Panmunjom(DMZ)
12.00 Lunch at Tongil Restaurant
14.30 Koryo Museum
16.00 Departure for Pyongyang

22ⁿᵈ – 23ᵗʰ April
International Conference on Finance

24ᵗʰ April
09:30 Pyongyang university of foreign languages
11:00 Taedongang Beer Mill
14.30 Meeting with the officials of Korean Narae Trade
17.00 Tour on the ship <Okryu No. 1>

25ᵗʰ
08.30 Departure for the airport
10.15 Take-off

ACT IV

2018 LOW: $3,200

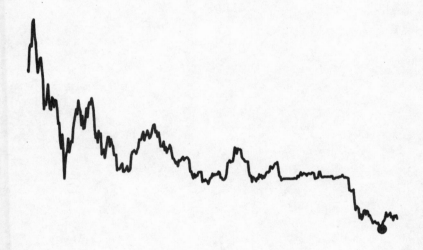

CHAPTER 20

In the summer of 2018, Jan Cerato went to a brewery in northern Calgary for an event for Liber T Token, a coin like one of the countless made through the Ethereum network. Its team was selling the token to fund a social movement championing individual freedom and rights — a cause to which many cryptocurrency enthusiasts would be partial, for one survey showed almost half of all Bitcoin holders considered themselves libertarians. Hours before the event, Jan, wearing his Bitcoin hat and Bitcoin T-shirt, stood in the brewery's cavernous event space — big enough for 144 people, the beer maker said — chatting with a Liber T team member, Basil, a bespectacled, peppery man of few words.

"How excited are you about this?" Jan smiled widely.

"Really excited. We're doing a launch today." Basil flashed around a brochure for Liber T. "We're starting a political party," he added, talking about one of the projects to be funded by the token sale.

"Let's see that token." Jan referred to the brochure. "That's the one we designed right here on the cover." His company had apparently had a hand in the logo. "It looks amazing," Jan said of the Liber T Token design.

"That's right," Basil said. "Let's be the change."

"Let's be the change." Jan repeated Basil's words, saying them louder and with more emphasis.

People in cryptocurrency and blockchain hold a wide range of views, but those who prize individual rights are overrepresented and often the most prominent. It's not hard to see why. As cryptocurrency gained mainstream attention and exploded in price, in a moment of vindication, it was the very early adopters, many of whom on society's fringes, who found themselves millionaires, magnates, and barons. WikiLeaks, which turned to Bitcoin after payment platforms banned it, said it made returns as high as 50,000 percent. Such successes simply reinforced the non-conformist, anti-authoritarian belief that drove Bitcoin in the first place. The early investor Roger Ver — noted for snapping up the prized one-word domain Bitcoin .com — had planned to start his own country, with laws that focused on individual rights. It was an idea explored by many others in some form, and not that different from what Liber T Token was trying to do.

As Jan and Basil spoke, in the background of the brewery, across from the steel vats, a musician set up drums against a rustic, timber panel. A little in front of it stood a projection banner for the big presentation that night. About a half dozen people were milling around. "What a beautiful facility, all kinds of space for everyone," Jan said, standing next to a billiards table. A day earlier, he had posted on social media that he wanted to hire 50 to 100 people within the year. In the brewery, Jan said, "It's going to be a great night of networking, marketing, talking about the whole Liber T coin movement."

The beer-making house, Railyard Brewing, was near the airport, not far from where my business partner, Winsor Hoang, lived.

The brewery's founders had crossed many train tracks when they were driving to scout locations, and it was when they stopped at a railway crossing that the name came up. "As we're sitting there one day waiting for one of the freight trains to go by . . . why not 'Railyard'?" its co-owner Brandon Fortes told media. Those tracks cutting through the city had a special meaning to the West. A lot of the oil produced in the region was shipped on the tracks, but moreover, rail had had a hand in the birth of the city. Fortes said of the tracks: "Ties our economy. Ties our culture. From there we were inspired." It was only in 1884, when the tracks and spikes came to the West, that the ragtag frontier community was formally incorporated into a town. And like many communities anticipating the rail, it experienced a period of wild land speculation, for real estate near a train station was big money. Investment interest was so rife, the railway company carefully guarded the secret of where exactly the train was going to stop when it came to town. But that did not stop the rush to buy real estate in hopes its price would rise. With the sales came the buildings on top of the land, sometimes sprouted for no reason other than the fact that a railway was coming. So parts of the city began empty, like a bubble.

As the night went on, the Liber T team member Brad Carrigan walked to a large television bearing the project's stylized *T* logo to address attendees. He stood one leg crossed in front of the other, leaning against a wooden shelf that held PlayStation games. Graffiti lined the wall behind him. Brad was a man of multitudes, having been a musician, political candidate, and, long ago, author of a book about what he described as the year 2012's "Great Revealing." Aside from the political party, the Liber T Token team wanted to use the money raised to fund a public-education wing that would focus on health and wellness, a news network for coverage in line with its views, and an online portal for "common-law information that informs and protects our individual rights and freedoms." One Liber T Token was 25 cents, and the team hoped to raise $129 million. It was a big event. There was to be a buffet dinner, a disc jockey, live music, and dancing. The invitation had "Gala" in big, gold, cursive font.

Among the gathered was another Liber T team member, Jan Cerato's business partner Alex Jackson, and just in front of him was Jan himself. But the two had not worked together for weeks, by Jan's estimation. Someone close to the duo told me, "There was a lot of power struggle between the two, in terms of who is actually leading the circus." Then there was a curious incident involving some $60,000, which went as all curious incidents involving some $60,000 would go. That amount was supposed to be sent to Dave Bradley, who supplied the Bitcoin the duo was selling. While there is dispute about what exactly happened and who exactly was responsible, all acknowledge that the money that was supposed to go to Dave did not make it to him. Dave did not actively pursue it. For an old-school Bitcoiner who had held cryptocurrency since at least early 2013, and who seemed to have a hand in nearly every related venture in the city, it wasn't worth the effort. But for Jan and Alex, for a partnership formed only in mid-2017 when Bitcoin was raging, that friendship of summer fractured further under the weight of it all. The partnership had lasted through the winter, but that was it. Jan and Alex had been doing business separately.

Perhaps that dispute lingered on Jan's mind as he sat at a table just in front of Alex. As the drinks flowed at the brewery, Jan pulled up a picture he had made from a photo of Alex and sent it out. Jan did not send it to his former business partner.

The picture featured Alex looking into the camera against a white background. Over it were red, capitalized words accusing Alex and his wife of a crime. I have never heard anyone else make that allegation, and Alex himself flatly denied it. Without providing any evidence other than a largely illegible invoice, Jan said Alex and his wife had "SCAMMED" people.

It is unclear how many people received that photo, but the Oleum contractor Elias Ahonen was one of them, and he promptly forwarded it to Alex. While I do not have Jan's account of that day directly from him, I do have a recording of a call and a screenshot of a text exchange he had with Elias, in which he admitted to sending the picture. As well, Alex provided me with what he said were screenshots of text exchanges he had with Jan, in which the latter admitted to the action.

Calling it a "meme," Jan later recalled to Elias he had shown and discussed that picture with others, including Dave — who Jan said told him not to send it — before sending it, which points to some preparation. Yet it was not a technically difficult image-editing job and had been done with the smartphone app PicJointer. It is unclear how spur of the moment the sending was, whether when Jan woke up that day, he expected others to be receiving that disparaging picture of Alex when the man was standing almost right next to him, unaware. Jan certainly did not expect what happened next.

Alex said he pulled out his phone to show Jan the message, holding it in front of his face. In his later text conversation with Elias, Jan confirmed the substance of that interaction. Alex said of Jan: "He looked like a child that got his hands caught in the cookie jar, you know. I looked at him, and I'm like, 'It's funny that you think you're just going to send out all the pictures and stuff of me, and not think anyone's going to frickin' do it — you know, tell me about it.'"

Jan then tried to embrace Alex, according to the latter, who described it as "stab you in the back, and then try to hug you, so that he can stab you in the back again." Alex rejected the gesture. "I told him to go fuck himself. I'm like, 'No, I'm not going to fucking touch you. Are you kidding me?'" Alex said that, days later, he confronted Jan at his house after a second person forwarded him that picture, and the man apologized.

Yet the dispute intensified nonetheless. Someone close to Jan posted in a group chat claiming all sorts of bad conduct on the part of Alex. There was no evidence provided. It was even unclear if that someone had actually posted the message or was being impersonated, and I therefore withhold the person's name. Then Jan had a legal letter to his former business partner drafted through a most curious choice of lawyer — years earlier, the attorney Cameron Bally had sued Jan over a debt; it was more than half a year after the letter to Alex that the hired collection agency said the amount was paid. Jan also told others, without citing any proof, that police had an active case against Alex for "cyber crimes," and that his former business partner was "desperately" trying to obtain the home addresses of his clients. Alex provided a recording of a conversation he said he had with a policeman, who said he was not under any investigation. Alex said of Jan: "Twelve years ago, I'd smash his fucking toes in. Legit. I'm not even joking. I'm not even joking. . . . I drilled holes for a living back in the day."

That night of the Liber T event, amid the sea of high tables fashioned after cable spools, with the smell of barley in the air, whatever hope there had been of mending the duo's fractured partnership was wiped away. "Salt and pepper," as Jan had described them, was no more and nevermore, and the man was set on a much lonelier path in the cryptocurrency Wild West. That heralded something dark, for the markets are an exhausting and perilous thing to ride, like an unbroken horse.

CHAPTER 21

Two weeks after the Liber T Token event was the Bitcoin Rodeo conference by Steve Carter's Oleum startup. Organizers had their own beer brand just for the occasion, the Bitcoin Buckaroo Brew. A faceless cowboy rides a raging bull on its label, one hand on the reins and the other brandishing a physical bitcoin. The event was held in the middle of downtown Calgary at the Palace Theatre performing hall, so named because it had opened as a "movie palace" in 1921, with Renaissance-style Corinthian pilasters and a red tapestry-brick facade, back when seeing a film was a grand affair.

It was that time of year again, the Stampede, when the city held a ten-day celebration of its western roots. Riders came in from all over the world to mount bulls and race horse-wagons at an arena practically right next to Cowboys Casino. Spectators came from all over the world as well, to watch those cowboys almost kill themselves. It was the Wimbledon of the West. Every restaurant patio, every outdoor event had bales of hay strewn around. Every major company held its own Stampede party. Executives showed up in Stetson hats, riding boots, big belt buckles, and flannel shirts. Some companies even custom-made their own western attire, and everyone spent the week hopping the open bars that somehow every party seemed to have. The coffee meetings, phone conferences, contracts, and signatures of more sober times traced their lineages to the hugs and clinked beer glasses of the Stampede. And what a show it was, for the festivities swung with the markets, as if giving thanks to some patron deity — St. Billiam of the Blue Barrels or whatever. Usually displays of extravagance and excess, the parties had been increasingly muted as companies cut back due to the oil crash, but in 2018 the barrels had boomed ever so slightly after the bust, and the pride of the West showed.

"We had a bit of a night last night," the Bitcoin YouTuber Ben Perrin said as he walked down the street with a fellow practitioner, Kenn Bosak, a man with a baseball cap, red beard, and twinkly eyes. The duo ran into Jan Cerato, who wore a Bitcoin hat and had a cryptocurrency pendant around his neck. He was wearing white-framed sunglasses and dark gloves and was carrying a pale box full of something. It seemed heavy, for his biceps bulged with the strain.

Jan had parked his green Jeep outside the Palace Theatre, adorned with the orange Bitcoin logo, hauling a trailer that contained a sort of tiny living room. He called it the country's "first mobile Bitcoin office," and its white interior walls were covered with cryptocurrency stickers. Jan gave Kenn a microphone, and the latter pumped his fist and asked random passersby: "Do you know what Bitcoin is? Do you know what Bitcoin is?"

The trio laughed. All were wearing some sort of Bitcoin T-shirt. Ben's and Kenn's referenced the mysterious creator Satoshi Nakamoto. Ben's, in particular, mocked the Australian computer scientist Craig Wright, the most prominent but unproven and widely disputed claimant to the identity of Bitcoin's inventor. Jan's black T-shirt was the most interesting: "If anyone tells you Bitcoin is a scam, stop talking to them. You don't need that kind of negativity in your life" — which could be interpreted as an encouragement to seek easy and comfortable experiences and avoid challenges to one's world view. It was almost a satire.

On that sunny summer day, beneath all that mirth and merriment of the Bitcoin Rodeo lay the ugly nakedness of an uncomfortable truth: from its peak, Bitcoin had fallen two-thirds to $6,700. The bull raged only on the beer labels.

The whaleclub that Jan promoted had been disquiet. It's unclear how many investors there were, but Jan would publicly peg that number at no less than 20, and statements sent to them indicated there were 34. According to statements sent to one investor, the whaleclub's "profits" had been in the negative and sinking further week after week, reaching as much as -69 percent.

In writing this book, I've spoken to eight investors, at least six of whom had reached out to Jan about the whaleclub funds in some way as prices fell. While Jan would later say he had not been the one leading the whaleclub, he would acknowledge that he had promoted it to potential investors, that he was "the person my people trusted," and that his role had been to "oversee" the operation "so we could report to the members on a monthly basis."

The prospect of losing money is to be expected for any investment, to be sure. The fact that it is happening is not a reflection of any ill intention on the part of whoever manages the money. For his part, Jan would later say that none of the investors from the whaleclub had been upset, that any complaints had come only from "all the jealous people." He would say, "I'm successful, 'cause I raised money, 'cause I got people behind me, 'cause people invested in me," and that the "jealous people" had badmouthed the whaleclub "'cause they can't get any money."

Lannie Clarkson, however, who was no longer working for Jan as his assistant, said she had been getting calls from whale-club investors. "They were asking me if I still worked with Jan and if I knew how to get a hold of him." I wasn't able to get more details from her, but at least one investor said he had trouble getting in touch with Jan. Jan also lashed out at that investor, according to a text exchange shown to me by his former business partner Alex Jackson. While I may never know the full context of the conversation, and Jan did not address the matters when I brought it up to him, I have verified with the investor himself the substance of what Jan allegedly said:

"Your [sic] still around? The hells angels havent got a hold of you yet? Its [sic] just a matter of time! Good luck with your big mouth!

"Cant wait to see you covered in duct tape with the bikers cocks in your big mouth, were [sic] gonna put those pics up on the telegram for everyone to see what a rat looks like.

"Quit talking to me, fuck off forever, we never want to see or hear your name again!! You clear on that??"

It must have been a stressful time.

While Jan had publicly said, "I became an investor when I was 28 years old," he later said in a blog post, "I know nothing about the investing world." Jan's specialty was marketing. He had studied web design and visual communications in college. One time, Jan seemed to have no idea to whom some money in the whaleclub belonged. "We got 1.07 [bitcoins] in the whale wallet whose funds are they?" Jan had asked his team.

"Not from me," Kirk Matthews responded, and those 1.07 bitcoins were never brought up again in the Telegram chat.

Throughout the downturn of 2018, Jan was still traveling widely, but at one point, he put his house up on the rental plat-form Airbnb.

No stress showed at the Bitcoin Rodeo, of course, where Jan was having a lot of fun, viewing it as an "honor" to meet people "from all around the world." He was grateful to a friend for "being part of the energy." He believed he had learned a lot, going around taking copious pictures inside the Palace Theatre, where all the day drinking under the bright signs amid the darkness made it seem like a nightclub. Jan even did a livestream, walking around with his selfie-stick, cajoling people to talk to the camera — "We've got lovely ladies in the house; say hi, girls!" — describing the attendees as "on fire" and the event as "tremendously powerful."

Indeed, Oleum's Dave Bradley and gang had pulled out all the stops. They flew in the author Saifedean Ammous, who had written *The Bitcoin Standard*, popular among a group that believed in Bitcoin maximalism — that only the first crypto-currency had staying power. There was free sushi for lunch. YouTubers descended upon the Bitcoin Rodeo, some of whom were streaming directly from the event. Among them was even a nine-year-old, the "Crypto Coin Kid." Outside, in the middle of downtown, the organizers doubled their beasts of burden. In addition to the pony Dave had talked about, there also stood a donkey. Their names were Moon and Charlie, and they wore cowboy hats and striped and checkered kerchiefs around their necks. They looked like little humans.

But, of course, you can only dress up a donkey so much.

CHAPTER 22

Helping Oleum sell tickets, Jan Cerato had been telling people the Bitcoin Rodeo was "our" event and that "we've got all kinds of action happening" and thanked people for going. It was consistent with how he often spoke, although he did not always explain to what exactly the plural pronouns referred. In one of Jan's mass emails on the rodeo, he said he had hot money-making investment advice and was "giving away the Tips during this exclusive Event live." He added he would reveal "The Imminent Trigger Event That May Send Bitcoin to $100,000." But Jan was not listed as a speaker at the conference. He parked his Jeep and trailer outside, advertising his cryptocurrency coaching, selling T-shirts, hats, and pendants such as the one he wore.

I saw Jan inside the Palace Theatre. We shook hands but did not say much, although a week later he texted to ask for introductions to cryptocurrency miners in Vancouver. Many interactions were similar that day as I navigated the three stories of the theater, filled with people I didn't know well but had either seen before or had seen me before, many of them a few Bitcoin Buckaroo Brews in.

There was, in fact, a lot to be said. The markets had moved in a way none of us had hoped or expected. Behind every handshake and smile was a gaping wound. For me, there was also a feeling of powerlessness, a vulnerability derived from bewilderment. Why had Bitcoin fallen so much? Ask ten pundits, you could hear ten different reasons, but those same sages had all made prodigious price predictions — $30,000 per bitcoin by 2018, for example — that now bordered on the ridiculous. I would know, for that prediction was mine, made on a Reuters television segment in which I strutted like some dunghill rooster. Those words had come out breezy. Now they returned heavy. Cheap talk had become expensive. I had based that prediction on what I thought were smart analysts, such as the widely followed and highly bullish Thomas Lee, who ended up so famously and catastrophically wrong, he had no corner into which to back, saying only the market was valuing Bitcoin incorrectly. I thought back to when I covered the oil markets at Reuters. One lesson from there had taken me a long time to truly appreciate.

A commonly cited reason for why oil is up or down is the movement of the U.S. dollar, because barrels are denominated in greenbacks. But for the same reason, one commonly cited factor for the rise and fall of the U.S. dollar is the swing of oil prices. In a way, when people comment on finance, whoever they may be, they often exemplify what George R.R. Martin repeatedly writes in the fantasy series that begins with *A Game of Thrones*: "Words are wind." The markets do not move without reason, that is for sure, but sometimes it is hubris to think we know what that reason is. The only certainty is that, like the dark-winged pigeons bearing bad news, the Bitcoin price drop was a herald for even darker things.

Because my company had more electricity than we could use, another revenue stream, apart from mining with our own machines, was to host others'. But amid the downturn, one such client — an Australian who had made a fortune betting on the battery element lithium and now spent part of his time building orphanages in Nepal — defaulted on tens of thousands of dollars' worth of payment. I took his machines, but they were worth so little now, some in China sold them by the kilogram. Citing prices, a major international player pulled out of talks to partner on a massive expansion of my mining facility, a million-dollar deal the subject of numerous long-distance calls. My company wasn't growing as I had hoped, and its profit diminished by the day.

After the Bitcoin Rodeo's formal events, we partied under a big tent downtown, set up all western-like just for the Stampede. I met the team of Toronto's 3iQ, an investment manager that would in 2021 launch a Bitcoin exchange-traded fund — a product backed by the cryptocurrency, listed on the stock market. I had a beer or two. It was good, and so was the live music. The air smelled of straw and spilled alcohol. But there was an under-current of sordidness that tugged at me. Bitcoin was still much higher than at any time when I bought, and my personal crypto-currency holdings still sat at the comfortable six digits, but I had not even bought a rodeo ticket. I had been granted access through one of the sponsors, which really was no different from sneaking in. Everyone did it. I don't think I know a single person who actually paid for the event. Across the cryptocurrency world, there was a collective recognition that we were all squeezed flat like turds under a wagon wheel. All the optimism of the years, the opulence and the carefree nonchalance of living large, they had gone by like a fading breath. In South Korea, where one cryptocurrency conference had come with an open-bar pool party teeming with hired models — recruited, perhaps, because cryptocurrency by itself did not tend to attract the attractive — millennials who lost money were killing themselves. What do you expect, though, when one in five investors internationally bought cryptocurrency with borrowed money?

I never thought of joining those ill-fated Koreans, of course. I had no debt, and I still had yet to read the last Harry Potter story — so much to live for. I had also been through that before, in 2013, and had been rewarded for keeping faith, albeit shakily. But the greatest folly of any investor is to believe past performance is any indication of the future. Every coin flip, after all, is its own independent event, unaffected by how many heads or tails precede it. What if Bitcoin did not bounce back this time? What if, all this time, we had all just been hitting our heads with each other's heads? The dead Koreans lingered long on my mind, those fortune seekers crossing into the new world only to find the plump promises were not to be. I felt a part of me was missing.

Lots of people in cryptocurrency called themselves early investors. The term is vague and subjective and easily applied, yet ironically it was a good calling card. Not only was that an indication of foresight, it was also a sure marker of wealth, important in a field in which objective metrics for screening people were few. Cryptocurrency folks came from everywhere, and there was no expectation for a blockchain degree or anything like that. For all the idealism and noble ambitions of that new world, many had stood propped up by their money, at least in some small way — the knowledge that they had it and the confidence that granted. It was as if wealth were a wall behind their backs, thick and redbrick, its foundation firm. Now that lay broken.

I consider myself a hardy man. At one point in my life, in an event that will perhaps be depicted in another book, I literally crawled through mud with machine-gun fire over my head. I'm capable of withstanding many different kinds of punishment, even the band Limp Bizkit. But that day, amid the revelry downtown, I keenly felt the sort of exhaustion that was the price of hubris. I was so scrambled, I could have been served with bacon. I excused myself and left early.

Before I was home, though, I was outside the Palace Theatre, where the miniature equine duo Moon and Charlie, cute as they were, had brought me little joy. Earlier, outside the theater, I saw Oleum's Steve Carter, wearing a button-down shirt that looked expensive, although I wasn't sure if he saw me. By then, he had a new office, towering some seventeen stories over downtown in the same sleek, tan building that housed the U.K. oil company BP, which you know is fancy because there's a fountain in its lobby. Steve did not know when, but he had an inkling, a foreboding anticipation, that trouble — albeit a different sort — was coming for him as well.

CHAPTER 23

Oleum's office was airy and looked even more so because of its glass doors. Anyone outside could see everything inside with all its yellowy tinge. The space could fit far more than Oleum's core staff, no more than half a dozen people, and sometimes the company would hold public events there with wine and cheese. It was prime real estate, and Oleum's office was on the seventeenth floor. Looking out of his window, Steve could see no people, only the shifting sun upon the fancy hotels all around. Up so high, a man might feel unassailable, like a sharpshooter in a hilltop rifle pit. Yet trouble knocked all the same. That Stampede, just three days after the Bitcoin Rodeo had begun, Steve got a visitor.

"Gifted, unpredictable," and a "demon," as described by sports publications, the man had been a professional hockey player and he was built like one, almost six feet tall and 180 pounds of pure muscle. The 36-year-old visitor was actually three months younger than Steve, but he was taller by almost a full head. If he wanted, he could have been an imposing man.

When Steve looked at the visitor, he might have felt a certain familiarity. While Steve had never met the man before him, he'd seen that powerful jaw, those wide shoulders, and that trunk-like neck on another man — one with whom Steve had worked closely on Oleum before falling out. The visitor's name was Jade Galbraith, and he held in his hand a lawsuit from the oilman Dale Galbraith that he was to serve on the Oleum founder. The son bore the feud of the father, and he had come to deliver it unto Steve.

In Oleum's early days, Dale had come to believe Steve unprofessional in running a business and ignorant about oil. Steve denied the allegations and instead accused Dale of not delivering on promised funding and corporate support, saying it was the oilman who had been difficult. Whatever the case, the two men had clashed, and that clash escalated. In Dale's lawsuit — disputed by Oleum and untested before court — he claimed about half a million dollars, saying Steve and his team had used "elusive and damaging tactics" to kick him out of the company "in an unlawful manner by secretly and subversively" altering Oleum's corporate documents.

Earlier that day, a short walk away at a barbecue by a local Bitcoin exchange platform, where there was a lucky draw for Ultimate Fighting Championship tickets, Dale's son Jade had served Steve's business partner Dave Bradley with the same lawsuit. Unlike for Steve, that was done publicly, and Dave was left explaining to everyone what had just happened.

Delivering a lawsuit is awkward for both sides, so much so that the job is often outsourced to professional process servers. "You need to understand: you're not exactly bringing them the winnings of the Lotto 6/49," one server told *Vice*. In fact, many try to avoid that, and serving a lawsuit is often a quest in itself. The musician Kanye West, for example, was once served via a Nordstrom gift box. Jade had offhandedly thought he might have to resort to something like that, too, if he had trouble serving Steve. Jade had heard a lot about staging accidents to get a respondent's attention, "funny things like guys falling off a bike in front of guys." Before he went to the BP tower, Jade, not above "wigs and stuff," had joked with his father that he might have to change his appearance.

That is, of course, usually the stuff only of movies. While Jade had been "pretty pissed off" that, in his view, he had locked eyes with Steve and had knocked on the glass door and waited for fifteen minutes before the man came, the service of the papers went largely without incident.

Steve, for his part, did not make any note of the man in jeans, a hoodie, and a ball cap before him and scarcely remembered the interaction. Oleum had been Jade's first time serving, and his heart rate had gone up a bit in what was in his view "not a good excitement." For Dave, amid the smell of burgers in the air, Jade had even defaulted to his courtesies and said sorry. Jade remembered everything vividly. Steve, on the other hand — in business attire and doing business things like talking on the phone and typing on his computer for the fifteen minutes Jade said he waited — had been served before. And ever since he and Dale had clashed, Steve had been expecting a lawsuit. That day, as Steve opened the door to Jade, it was as if a grown bull was watching a knobbly kneed calf take its first steps.

Steve took the papers from Jade, and he read them. "Oh, okay, well, we've got to deal with it," he thought.

Oleum would attract three more lawsuits. A video-production company, a printing firm, and the blockchain consultant Elias Ahonen's company, Token Valley, separately sued Oleum for what they each said was lack of payment, which Oleum denied. The video producer, Decision Theory Media, had made for Oleum dramatic segments of galloping horses, cowboys, slow-motion bull-riding, and rushes of equine herds upon the prairie plains seen from up high, like from a helicopter. It was the firm hired to promote the Bitcoin Rodeo, which was supposed to put the region "on the map in the crypto world," billed as the "most important Bitcoin and blockchain conference the city of Calgary has ever seen!"

As Oleum's glass door closed, and Steve walked back inside his office after receiving Dale's lawsuit, Bitcoin was tumbling. It would end the day at around $6,200, down 7 percent since the beginning of the conference whose mood had been described by Jan Cerato as "bananas." And the pain was only beginning. As the philosopher Homer — the American one — points out in *The Simpsons Movie*, things are never the worst ever; they're just the worst "so far."

*The following is extracted from the actual document. It has been selec-
tively excerpted for length, but is otherwise unedited. Figures are in
Canadian dollars. The defendants deny all of the allegations. They say
that the plaintiff, Dale Galbraith, had no stake in the business in the
first place, as claimed. The defendants say that stake was contingent on
Dale's provision of certain funds and services, commitments on which he
allegedly never delivered. The matter remains untested before court.*

**Provincial Court of Alberta
(Civil)
Dale Galbraith
Ideation Group Inc. and Catch Ventures Inc.**

Plaintiff(s)

**and
Stephen Paul Carter, David O'Connor, David Bradley
and
Oleum Capital Inc.**   **Defendant(s)**
Oleum Capital Holdings Inc.

Civil Claim

The Plaintiff Claims from the Defendant $ <u>Total $504,700 = 24,700</u>
<u>(advanced money, legal & corporate) + $480,000 for Corp Total includes plain-</u>
<u>tiffs rightful 40% ownership in Oleum Capital Holdings Inc. & Oleum Capital</u>
<u>Inc.</u> and costs of this action.

The reasons for the Claim are:

That subsequent to filing the corporate documents and providing same to the
defendants, the defendants began elusive and damaging tactics, which excluded
the plaintiff from advancing the agreement between the plaintiff and defendants. This action included secretly advancing the corporation's initiatives.

That the defendants did willfully and knowingly thwart all efforts by the plaintiff to be part of the corporation and that the defendants did act in an unlawful
manner by secretly and subversively causing the corporate documents of Oleum
Capital Inc. to be altered without the consent or knowledge of the directors or
executive of the Company.

That the defendants have benefitted substantially at the expense and exclusion
of the plaintiff, without honouring the original Agreement.

ACT V

2019 LOW: $3,400

CHAPTER 24

It was a drab November evening when Jan Cerato held his 61st meetup, for which fifteen people had registered. The light had long left the sky, where clouds drifted with a southern wind. The streets lay gray with old snow, and the air lingered in the subzero. It seemed the sort of wearisome midweek day that fades from memory after it passes. Jan held his meetup in the same room in the casino restaurant, named after the Kabuki style of Japanese dance-drama. Outside hung the same picture of the riding samurai, his face shrouded like the Nazgûl of *The Lord of the Rings*, his mount gray as driftwood. Soy sauce was served in the same Buddha-shaped bottle. Jan promoted his Bitcoin-selling business. "Crypto is going to be the absolute, defining, digital matter kind of thing in the future of our lives," he said. "This is a velocity that's blossoming." Jan added that cryptocurrency "can't be regulated and controlled by anyone but you" and has an "impervious shield" against the government. He did not say anything he had not already said. But that night was not like any other. That night, in attendance, was someone from the Alberta Securities Commission.

It is unclear who from the regulator was there or why. But looking at the expense report and receipt, which I've obtained via a freedom-of-information request, it appears that person ate healthily — the amount spent was the exact price of a salad, poke, or sashimi bowl — and had good taste, for each would have been delicious. The staffer also likely had undying loyalty for the commission and desire to save it money, for the tip was a miserly 10 percent on a bill that was only half the maximum the commission allowed for dinner. That person was probably dedicated and wanted to leave no stone unturned, for there is an almost saintly patience that can be inferred from getting the bill only near the end of the four-hour session. It also appears that whatever task at hand had to be important, for Jan livestreamed a great many of his meetups and also released the audio on his *JanCity* podcast, complete with prerecorded and thunderous applause and cheers added to the beginning — if the commission staffer's objective was merely to take in the contents of Jan's talk, going down to the event in person was unnecessary. What is beyond guesswork, though, glaringly clear from the expense report, is that the employee had come from the commission's enforcement unit and was there for business. Speaking in that casino that night, Jan might not yet have known it, but the local cryptocurrency scene had attracted the attention of people whose job it was to pay attention. The saloon floor had become still, and on it, grinding, rattling across, the sound of spurs. The law had arrived to tame the wild.

It had come from the east.

In 1963, a young French-Canadian couple got married in Shawinigan, Quebec. The husband was a doctor, and the couple soon left for the United States for his specialized further studies. So Louise Panneton was born in New York City in 1969. The Pannetons later moved to Quebec City, the capital of the French-speaking province. Louise went to law school there. Then came graduate school and marriage in Montreal. Louise was 27, and her husband, 28. The couple went on to have three children.

In the beginning, Louise worked in the finance industry in the private sector, but it was not her true calling. Her graduate thesis, "L'obligation d'information du médecin et son impact sur la vie de couple," was on balancing doctor-patient confidentiality with the well-being of the sick person's intimate partner, a well-written and non-jargony tome on ethics in public service — healthcare in Canada being largely in the government's hands. In 2006, after at least five years in the private sector, working first for a mutual-fund manager and then an insurance company, Louise joined the civil service, becoming an investigator for the Autorité des marchés financiers, Quebec's securities regulator.

For nearly seven years, Louise worked for the regulator, headquartered in a 47-story downtown monolith, a building for which business interests and structural reality had reined in artistic ambition. Louise executed search warrants, initiated freeze and cease-trade orders, and worked closely with police. She questioned witnesses. She wrote investigative reports. She assisted prosecutors during hearings and trials. The work was a drastic change from what Louise previously did. Then, in 2013, came another drastic change. Louise left her job and left Montreal, joining the Alberta Securities Commission in Calgary.

Louise never responded to my attempts to contact her, so I do not know why she moved. It certainly seemed abrupt. Aside from being born in New York, over which she had no choice, she had spent nearly her entire life in Quebec. Louise even spoke English with a French-Canadian accent. But I like to think the specific explanation doesn't matter. Underneath all the motivations and rationales of why people head west, it's all the same reason. The West simply has a way of reaching out to people, beckoning them.

As 2018 marched toward and into winter, Louise trained her crosshairs on Jan. People across the Calgary cryptocurrency scene were contacted by the commission — emails, phone calls, a courier showing up at the door with a stern letter:

> Please find enclosed for service upon you a Summons with respect to an interview. . . . The investigation and this Summons are confidential and must not be divulged. . . . All communications of any nature and kind regarding the investigation and this summons are expressly restricted.

In a commission investigation, unlike a criminal one, people have fewer rights. You cannot remain silent, and the commission can legally restrict what you say publicly. There must have been at least 30 people given the summons, for I spoke to more than that many when I later looked into the matter, and I am just one man, while Louise worked with a colleague and had institutional muscle.

I reached out to that institutional muscle, too. I hobnobbed with the commission's people. I went to its conference, where due to what I assume was my prolificness in filing freedom-of-information requests, the commission's senior counsel recognized and approached me. I lunched with one of the commission's communications managers, who said it was a "pleasure" (and I must say the pan-roasted chicken breast with wilted baby kale was delicious). But despite my best efforts to pry out information — my case had been raised all the way to the executive director, I was told — the regulator defaulted to usual practice, saying it "will not comment on, or confirm the existence of, an investigation related to the parties noted."

Before the year was up, though, word had spread. People whispered. Some even reached out to the commission unsolicited. I later heard from multiple sources that Jan, who maintained his innocence, was under investigation. I would also learn more specific details from an unexpected source. In 2019, Jan would be sued by a local businessman with whom he'd worked, Jeremy Ostrowski, after the two had had a dispute, in an untested lawsuit that, while unrelated, revealed a lot about the commission case. Among the documents filed to court was a note Jan was said to have written to Louise. It showed that, in December of 2018, one and a half months after the commission enforcer attended Jan's meetup at the casino, the man himself got a "Summons to a Witness," for which he said he sought a lawyer and needed to "prepare our files for review."

CHAPTER 25

As the commission investigation was underway, Jan held a cryptocurrency conference in the southern portion of the city, a district with practically no history near the gravelly banks of the river Bow, bluntly named Quarry Park, which had for 50 years been used for exactly what its name suggests. It was Jan's second conference, after an earlier one that, according to him, had been of such note that it "made it to the financial news!!" — although the article he cited was not actual media coverage but a press release labeled "Partnership Content."

The date for the second summit was no doubt carefully chosen: January 3, 2019. Not only did it coincide with Bitcoin's so-called birthday, it was a significant one at that — ten years — ten years earlier, in the wake of the financial crisis, Satoshi Nakamoto had mined the Bitcoin Genesis Block. And over that decade, the idealistic, outsider mentality of the early adopters had increasingly come up against a wider world that was unlike them, yet which also wanted a part of the action. Shortly before this anniversary, news had leaked that Facebook was planning its own cryptocurrency, as the suits and regulation increasingly entered the fray.

At his conference, Jan laid out a cake and led attendees in singing "Happy birthday, dear Bitcoin," waving his hands as a conductor would direct an orchestra. Jan was not in his usual Bitcoin cap and Bitcoin T-shirt. Instead he was Conference Jan, donning the navy suit jacket he wore to such events and important business meetings. "Ten years, baby, ten years!" Jan clapped and whooped before cutting the cake.

If Jan was worried that day about the probe from the investigator Louise Panneton and the Alberta Securities Commission, he did not show it. The later unrelated lawsuit from the businessman Jeremy Ostrowski, which remains untested before court, would shed further light on that. Jeremy, a man with curly gray hair, intense eyes, and an equally intense dislike of Jan Cerato — which I took into account when considering the businessman's information — would say in court documents that the man had told him about the commission case, and that "Mr. Cerato implied that it was a laughable matter and that he was being unfairly targeted." Jan's alleged note to Louise, which Jeremy told the court the man had sent him, indicated that he had posted about the investigation on social media within a day of receiving his summons from the commission. At a later meetup at Cowboys Casino, livestreamed, Jan said:

> You think that because I do Bitcoin, I'm doing scams and fraud — I am not. I'm not one of those guys. I'm one of the good guys that's doing Bitcoin properly, helping the neighbors get secure, helping the neighbors do it properly. So, at the end of the day, keep in mind, there's many ways to do Bitcoin, but there is a positive, clean, normal way to do it, and there is also a negative world that exists out there on the web, and I don't even go there. In fact, I don't even know where to go because it's not an interest of mine, okay?

Jan also posted a motivational picture on Facebook. It appeared without context, and it was unclear to what it referred. But its words were stark, white on black: "Be a fucking wolf. Be a fucking lion. Take no shit. Set goals, smash them. Eat people's faces off. Be a better person. Show people who the fuck you are. Never apologize for being awesome. Stay the mother fucking [sic] course."

J an had a lot of experience dealing with legal issues. He had been sued at least a dozen times, mostly over money, and in at least three cases, the plaintiff had had a hard time serving him with the paperwork. When Jan did not pay his rent, his landlady said, three attempts to serve him with the paperwork failed, and she ended up "posting them to the front door." When Jan was accused of not paying his mortgage for a different property, a claim yet untested, the process server Jude Klym said in an affidavit he had to call after being unable to find Jan in person. "It was answered by a male saying that I had reached a head office and to leave a message," he said. "Jan Cerato called [back] from a blocked number and left a voice message saying that 'they' were away. . . . He wanted to know where my office was and he would come by and pick up." Klym said he called back, but Jan went silent.

When a local company sued Jan's marketing business for an unproven allegation of non-delivery of services, Brad Longeway the process server said he had a similarly difficult time. When he tried to approach Jan at his office, a man that Longeway believed to be Jan "did not answer and just looked at me," he said. Then the man said he wasn't Jan. "He then stood up and put his hand on my back to guide me toward the door." Longeway tried to hand him the document package. "He refused to take it, so I dropped it onto his feet." As Longeway stood outside that midsummer day, he said, he saw "the door open a little and the documents were then thrown out the door."

In such cases, what those suing can do is apply for "substitutional service," giving notice though a newspaper advertisement, email, or whatever method the court deems reasonable. If you're suing Jan, the process can become much easier once that hurdle is crossed. In about half of the instances in which he was sued, Jan mounted no defense, filing nothing to court or being absent for scheduled events, and was ruled against in default.

But then it gets difficult again. The Royal Bank of Canada had to resort to trying to garnish Jan's wages. A Philip Waldenberger hired a bailiff to enforce a judgment. The lawyer Cameron Bally — hired by Jan against Alex, but who had also sued Jan for some reason — had turned to a debt collector in what appeared to be a drawn-out, exhausting process. When the collection agency told the court the amount had been "paid in full," it had been more than seven years since the lawsuit was filed.

For the other half of the claims against Jan, none had been proven in court. Some were still ongoing and some had been seemingly abandoned by their proponents. The latter situation is not unusual. A lawsuit is expensive and time-consuming. It also saps one's energy. I have been to the courthouse multitudes of times to research this book, and I cannot overstate what a ghastly, hellish — and for the uninitiated, probably unnerving — experience each trip was. Go on a few of those trips, pay a few court fees, write a few affidavits, and stand in line a few times for two hours when you have only budgeted one, and you question whether you're really entitled to what you feel is your $3,935. Sometimes a person's will just gives out. Many had tried to sue Jan, and even without his having to do anything, many just faded away.

But the commission investigator Louise Panneton was not someone who fades away. As winter went on, Louise's email inbox lit up with Google alerts for keywords such as "money laundering" and "pump-and-dump." The latter refers to a sort of shady practice in which perpetrators artificially inflate the price of an investment and then sell all they have at a high — a tactic that had been increasingly linked to cryptocurrency. In addition to legal newsletters from Mondaq, Louise's inbox contained updates about cryptocurrencies such as the privacy-focused Zcash and the efficiency-centered Nano, which used to be called RaiBlocks, after the stone currency of the Micronesian island of Yap. Louise paid keen attention to her work. When you ignored her knock, what followed was the battering ram.

CHAPTER 26

Louise Panneton was, by all appearances, a no-nonsense person, her brown hair in a low-maintenance bob, shoes practical, and handshake warm and firm. She also believed deeply in her mastery of the art of extracting information. "Summonsing" and "questioning witnesses," in Louise's words, were cited as highlights when she described her job. Along with Dale Fisher — a cop-looking guy with a grandfatherly voice who had at one point been a member of the commission's FasTrac rapid-response team — Louise would question people from Jan's case in the regulator's office in a 23-story blue-steel downtown tower.

The building had been designed by bigshot eastern architects with environmental friendliness in mind and a "playful informality" to the facade that looked futuristic and bright. But on the inside, the commission, like many government institutions, exuded an air of age and imposition. According to one witness, Louise and Dale would sit behind an oval boardroom table featuring wood with navy blue inlay, a sort of gaudy '80s-esque décor, and the former would ask three questions for every one the latter did.

That was planned, when the duo decided beforehand who would be the "lead" and "secondary" questioners, as the commission called them. The secondary should not interrupt the lead's flow, nor should he bluntly point out anything she missed, according to the regulator's internal enforcement manual. Even with a "compelling reason," the secondary should "discreetly consult with the lead before intervening." Like what Vito tells Sonny and what Michael tells Fredo in *The Godfather*, Louise and Dale would never reveal too much to outsiders. Everything was to be scripted and smooth. "There are three elements of a successful interview: preparation, preparation, and preparation," the investigators were taught. Make no mistake: nothing in a commission interview is spontaneous. For a single witness, the thickness of the documentation Louise and Dale gathered is best described by stretching out thumb and index finger. When Louise asked the questions, it was as if she already knew the answers. Even when Louise asked personal questions like where people worked and where they went to school, the goal, according to the internal manual, was in part to "assist in relaxing the witness and ease him or her into the ensuing stages."

The commission takes no chances and is not your friend. The summons, which threatens legal consequences should witnesses not show up, is "usually preferable" to voluntary interviews, so "time and effort is not wasted because of false starts when a witness turns out to be uncooperative." Even if matters might break solicitor-client privilege, "the Director has instructed that the questions be asked." Louise and Dale were taught to "use everything we normally use when we speak with friends, family," to "use emotions," to "use humour," to use first names, and to be "empathetic more than sympathetic," according to internal training slides. Some people are motivated more by threats and fear of consequences, some more by kindness and compulsion to return a favor. The commission knows all can be pushed by manipulating both those aspects. Louise was particularly good at that, having a particular way of putting people at ease, witnesses told me.

All of that, that deliberate, thoughtful readiness, that steely purpose beneath the veil of warmth, went beyond the interview to the genesis of the entire investigation. Before Louise got a case, it was first vetted by the commission's assessment unit, and if the unit saw merit, then that was often an ironclad call. "Only rarely does Investigations unit not proceed with a file referred," reads the commission's internal manual. "When Investigations division receives a case for investigation, it anticipates that the matter may, at the conclusion of the investigation, be formally referred to the Litigation division. This premise is expected to be reflected in the planning of the investigation." The translation of all that bureaucratic speak is that, long before any interviews, long before any witnesses were summonsed, and long before that commission enforcer appeared at Jan's November meetup to eat a poke, salad, or sashimi bowl, unknown to the crypto man, a series of events involving him had already been set off, compounding by the day.

Jan soon felt the seriousness of the commission's case. Around that period, investors told me, Jan returned to them portions of their whaleclub contributions, ranging from one-third to full. Then there was the note that Jan allegedly wrote to Louise, filed to court in the later unrelated and untested lawsuit from the businessman Jeremy Ostrowski. It was presented as an email, dated three days after Jan's earlier conference, although it is unclear if it was ever sent. In that note, which came "from the Desk of: Jan G. Cerato," the man told Louise he had identified a major heavy hitter to represent him: Jeffrey Thom of McLeod Law, who had more than 40 years of experience fighting lawsuits at all levels in the West and in the Supreme Court, where the head of the commission's enforcement unit had clerked. A Queen's

Counsel, a title granted in certain Commonwealth countries to recognize outstanding legal achievement, Jeff also had particular experience with the commission, having defended many against cases brought by Louise and her associates. Jeff and Louise even worked in the same blue-steel tower, and he once successfully argued for the court to cover the legal fees of a man charged by the commission — the man had said he could not pay — the first time such a request was granted for a securities case. "If you want to put somebody in jail, you can't do it without competent legal counsel," Jeff told media at the time. So deeply did the Queen's Counsel believe in that, he had argued the issue for free.

Jan's alleged note showed he had also prepared a copy of it for another lawyer at McLeod, a younger man with less experience but who had an expertise that many like Jeff — admitted to the bar before the advent of the personal computer — might lack. The younger man called himself "Matt 'bitcoin' Burgoyne" on Twitter, where his profile picture was a beaming cartoon caricature. He spoke at local cryptocurrency events and headed McLeod Law's cryptocurrency division. Matt and Jeff had all the makings of a powerful team.

But it is unclear if they ever ended up fighting for Jan. In a later email, Jeff told me any dealings he "had" with "Jan Ceruto" were confidential, and declined to comment — a curious tense usage that suggests past interaction, but also a misspelling of the man's name that indicates unfamiliarity. Jeff would not confirm or deny if he had represented or was still representing Jan. Perhaps my manners offended Jeff, and he plainly did not want to talk to me, so I will not read anything into that. But Jeff's response is certainly uncommon in my experience with lawyers, especially if they are not representing someone. If that is the situation, they usually outright say so. Matt did not respond when I reached out.

Whatever the case, according to Jan's alleged letter to Louise, he had received a firm reminder of the gravity of the situation. Louise had asked Jan to take down any public mention of the commission, the note showed. Revealing too much about a commission investigation before it's concluded theoretically could carry a jail term. Despite invoking Jeff and Matt and McLeod Law, the bulk of Jan's note to Louise was markedly deferential, saying he could not attend a proposed date for a meeting:

> We respectfully ask for an extension to prepare our files for review. . . .
>
> With respect to the request of removing ASC [Alberta Securities Commission] from any blogs or associated Dec 20, 2018 [sic] we have complied with that request immediately and removed the reference. Our entire staff genuinely apologizes for any confusion that may have transpired. . . .
>
> I'm genuinely attentive to this matter and I am able to respond through email & regular mail, while travelling on my 2019 Lecturing schedule and fully cooperate going further with any correspondence.

In the note, Jan did not elaborate on what the "2019 Lecturing schedule" meant, but on the day it was dated, he hightailed it to Puerto Vallarta in western Mexico.

T he spiral sculpture sat on the north side of the esplanade, right beside one of the oldest hotels in town, near the edge of the sea. The bronze monument celebrates the new millennium and was inaugurated on Halloween in 2001. It rises from a base of turbulent primordial waters, from where life first sprang, ending at a sun and a pair of hands in prayer — the coming of Christ. Above it is Emperor Charlemagne, who united western Europe for the first time since the Romans, encircled in the fires of the first millennium's violence. Up farther is the ancient Mexican poet-king Nezahualcoyotl, his coppery face in decay — violence yet again. But the feathered snake Quetzalcóatl, god of wind and wisdom, ties the bleak second millennium to a brighter third — a woman reaching for a dove at the top of the sculpture. The artist had worked on it for two years. Jan surveyed the piece and summed up pithily: "One of those icon things, big statues that they have. What is that, a sea serpent or something like that?" Then he and his friend Joshua walked down the esplanade and saw someone in a monkey costume handing out flyers for a restaurant. "What's up? Who's this guy?" Jan said, before turning to Joshua. "Take a picture of us."

It was a grand month. Jan called his crew "Tequila Hunterz," saying they were "looking for some of the best tequila in Mexico." He wrote on Facebook: "we only drink Tequila, the water, pop, coffee are all a second choice when it comes to tequila we run around with a full bottle at all times!" In Jan's mind, they couldn't run short on the alcohol, or they would not be "doing it properly." He posted liberally on social media, often livestreaming his and his friends' walks around town. In one scene, Jan trained the camera on a bikini-clad woman on the beach facing away. "This one's for the boys back home right there," he said. "You see that? It's for you guys — little bum cheeks in the wind." In a place like that, a man can easily lose himself, insulate himself from whatever gloom lay back home. Across two borders and living large, there was no indication at all that the law and Louise were after him.

But never did Jan forget, the last day of 2018, when snow had dusted the mountains west, pale and smoky beneath the moon. It was just a week before Jan left for Mexico, when he made the announcement: "Bitcoin Investments is closing its business permanently today Dec 31, 2018. The founder Jan Cerato didn't want to close the business and stop pursuing his dreams but had no choice." Jan considered shutting down his weekly meetups as well, events he had undertaken with both pride and enthusiasm. "I will take a step back, and hopefully try new things again soon," he said. Jan's quest for the enchanted gold had led to "some bad ones" among the people he met — "some serious evil was going against me," he felt. Jan became "too devestated [sic]." That night, all through the ensuing darkness, the air was clear and the wind still upon the moonlit snow. Never did Jan forget, and never, likely, did he forgive.

CHAPTER 27

Sometimes, when you try to rise in the world, all that happens is you bump your fat head on the cold ceiling fan. When the Dwarven miners of Middle-earth love gold too much and dig too deep in the Misty Mountains, they find a Balrog fire demon that drives them from their kingdom. Other Dwarves in the Lonely Mountain mine and mine, and then their haul attracts the dragon Smaug, the inferno sweeping across the heavens, and the aftermath that smolders. Even in Mexico, according to Jan Cerato, trouble came for him as well. "The cops shake me down every day," Jan said when he was there, wearing a T-shirt tiled with faces of the Toronto rapper Drake, whose "Started from the Bottom" the marketer viewed as his theme song. "I'm just too flashy or something." Earlier, Jan had said that shirt was "creating looks everywhere we go!" Prosperity is a cruel beacon sometimes. As a dead Roman wrote in *Agamemnon*, "Whatever Fortune has raised on high, she lifts but to bring low."

As Bitcoin had risen, so too had the exchange platforms on which people deposit traditional money to buy cryptocurrency, or vice versa. In 2017, nearly $2 billion flowed through the QuadrigaCX platform founded by Gerald Cotten, who, of course, bought an airplane and a 51-foot sailboat named *The Gulliver*, presumably after the eighteenth-century book of fantastical tales.

With such massive inflows to exchanges came responsibility. The best platforms wielded that with care. But the field as a whole operated with little oversight, and exchanges were surprisingly to set up. Cryptocurrency transactions, of course, are also irreversible. All of that was not a good combination. Many exchanges had risen too much and too quickly, and I would realize that at the worst possible time.

Throughout Bitcoin's fall, I had to sell increasingly more of it to pay the bills for my company. And every time I did so, I could not help but think back to the one Bitcoin sale I'd done that was not on an exchange but in person, to my real-estate friend Curtis, back when one bitcoin was still a respectable $14,000. Because of the fall in prices, Curtis had effectively lost a lot of money. It is true that anyone can buy Bitcoin anywhere, and I could have sold anywhere. I hadn't charged Curtis a markup, and in fact, I hadn't even offered to sell. He had come to me. I like to think I took no more advantage than the Samaritan did of the traveler from Jerusalem. Curtis said he didn't blame me. But Curtis added that, on the day of the transaction, he had suppressed a voice at the back of his head that told him not to do it. I could not help but feel a little responsible. Then I started having trouble seeing my money.

I'd started using Gerry's Quadriga shortly after meeting him in 2014, but I eventually stopped. I flirted with different exchanges, settling on ezBtc, a rival of Gerry's, also based on the West Coast, founded by a former media worker, Dave Smillie, who called himself a "creative visionary" — which, in retrospect, should have been a red flag. Never trust a man who calls himself a creative visionary. Unknown to me at the time, ezBtc was mired in a million-dollar lawsuit. When I made five withdrawals totaling tens of thousands of dollars, every one of them got stuck. Amid the market downturn, that was the most uncomfortable and anxiety-inducing experience.

Eventually, I did get the money out, after more than one month of delay for one of the withdrawals and having to contact the founder Smillie himself. After purging from my mouth the sour taste of panic, I put on my journalist hat and went poking around. In another book, I write, "In times of crisis, I like to think, we are pared down to our most basic parts, our core functions." I held no sway over ezBtc, but I knew I had a different kind of power: I could tell the world what had happened. Eventually, I wrote in a regional publication that I'd discovered I was far from the only one who'd experienced this kind of obstacle in withdrawing money from ezBtc. In fact, some users said they never saw their money, even as — as I'd discovered — Smillie proposed to his girlfriend with a three-carat ring in a hotel's presidential suite and then had a wedding with gold cutlery. The ezBtc exchange was accused of owing more than $45 million, and soon the British Columbia Securities Commission started investigating. Smillie, who had told me he was committed to running a clean business and that others had "considerable misconceptions," seemingly went missing. His phone was disconnected. An email sent to him bounced. Social media profiles went dark.

So I asked B.C. Securities Commission Executive Director Peter Brady, a lawyer who joined the regulator in 2012, whether his investigators were able to reach Smillie.

"I actually can't tell you anything," he said during a phone interview.

So that was that.

Brady's commission did appear to have its hands full, though, governing the home to the world's first Bitcoin ATM.

The commission was also investigating another platform, Einstein Exchange, that ended up imploding and owing more than $12 million. Searching Brady's commission internally would produce more than 2,000 records, such as Word documents and spreadsheets related to cryptocurrency, an analyst told me. But Brady said the problems with bad actors were in no way unique to his regulator, and he was right. Regulators all over the world had been grappling with such issues and paying closer attention to the sector, hiring new people and sending existing ones for training, for the problems with exchanges, whatever forms they took, had been myriad.

When you say a cryptocurrency exchange platform has halted services after it lost millions of dollars in a hack, for example, you have to be specific. Which one are you talking about? Japan's Mt. Gox in 2014? South Korea's Youbit in 2017? Japan's Coincheck or Zaif in 2018? New Zealand's Cryptopia or Japan's Bitpoint in 2019? As well, there are the exchanges accused of high-level regulatory mishaps: two of the world's largest, Bitfinex and BitMEX, both founded in Hong Kong. While neither of their cases affected individual users, those that did, such as the hacks, often left people without any recourse. In the Mt. Gox saga, the collapse of what was once the world's biggest exchange, users' prospects of getting back their money were so dismal, a New York private-equity firm had offered to buy their claims for less than ten cents on the dollar.

Then there was, of course, Gerald Cotten's QuadrigaCX. Along with the large increase in transaction volume, Quadriga's external payment processors began having problems, and some $20 million ended up frozen by the Canadian Imperial Bank of Commerce. Two other payment processors of Quadriga were sued by U.S. authorities. One was accused of being part of a $165 million fraud. Another was accused of losing $851 million.

Throughout 2018, customers of the exchange reported delays when attempting to withdraw dollars.

Quadriga was at one point Canada's biggest exchange, and almost everyone in the country involved in cryptocurrency had had an account on it. As I watched all the exchanges' problems unfold, amid the rapid decline in the cryptocurrency market, I wondered if I had any coins still on Quadriga. I hadn't used it in more than a year, and I had forgotten all about it. I logged in to my account and saw that I had thirteen ethers on it, worth under $2,000 at the time. I made a mental note to withdraw them but did not deem it a priority. Then, as the story goes, Gerry died.

CHAPTER 28

Toward the end of 2018, soon after Gerry checked into a hotel in India, he complained of pain in his stomach. A physician from the hotel tended to him but did not do much. Gerry and his wife, in town for a charity honeymoon, a post-nuptial holiday during which they would also help build an orphanage, made their way to a private hospital. A feverish Gerry vomited ten times and had watery stool fifteen times. His back troubled him, and his abdomen felt cramped and hurting. The next day, Gerry's heart beat more and more laboriously. By sundown, he was declared dead.

The "CX" was short for "coin exchange," while a quadriga is a sort of Roman chariot — drawn by four horses abreast — that raced in the ancient games. Emblems of triumph, quadrigas are also ridden by the Roman mythical personifications of victory and fame. One such depiction is a statue atop Berlin's towering Brandenburg Gate, seized by Napoleon when he defeated what was then Prussia in 1806 and returned eight years later when Ernst von Pfuel's troops occupied Paris. Another rider of the quadriga is Apollo, who soars across the heavens every morning to bring the sun and disperse the dark, the deity who dawns the new day.

Gerry's wife-turned-widow, Jennifer Robertson, did not announce the news of his death for more than a month. In a way, that was not unexpected. Who would not anticipate the shockwaves the news would send, not just in the cryptocurrency realm but also the wider world? While Quadriga had had its share of problems, they were mostly contained in the insular cryptocurrency space. To the outside, the platform had been a shining star. It was a pioneer, one of Canada's oldest exchanges, operating when few even knew what a cryptocurrency was. At one point, it was even to become publicly traded. Now the god behind the chariot had fallen.

I took a nap and woke up groggy on a cold winter's day in early 2019. I hadn't been out of the apartment in almost three days, as the wretched ugliness of the season piled outside. The streets were like an unfinished painting, with so much white. Sometimes I wish I could be a bear, unconscious throughout the whole bitter period. I boiled water for tea and lazily thumbed through my emails. Then I saw a statement from Jennifer Robertson.

I had never been so awake in my life.

I was a fairly young man. At the time, I'd only ever been to one wedding and zero funerals. Apart from a great-grandfather I saw once when I was seven and an editor for whom I wrote one article in university, who had cancer at the time, Gerry was the first person I'd met to die. And his fall reflected the decline of something else. It had been a painful year in cryptocurrency. What had begun as an incremental slide had escalated to become a calamitous wreck. By early 2019, Bitcoin had seen prices as low as $3,200, down sharply from the brief height of $20,000 in December 2017. Taking into account the wider cryptocurrency market, more than $700 billion was lost in total.

Financial ruin swept the land, both personal and commercial. The U.S. Department of Justice started investigating whether the rally leading up to the 2017 high had been the result of price manipulation. For all of us in that new world, it was as if we had looked the goddess Fortuna in the eye, said, "Please beat me," and then handed her the stick.

One of the first things I did when I heard the news of Gerry's death was to try to log in to my Quadriga account to withdraw my thirteen ethers. The request went through, but the next day, the site went down, and I never saw my coins. Quadriga had collapsed quickly after the news of Gerry's death. His widow said Gerry alone held the password to the platform's cryptocurrency. Roughly 115,000 users had more than $140 million in coins stuck. Quadriga entered bankruptcy proceedings.

The biggest publicly known Quadriga user at the time, a Canadian software engineer by the name of Tong Zou, wasn't even a big cryptocurrency enthusiast. Living in the United States, Zou had been in the process of moving back home, and he bought Bitcoin in greenbacks and immediately sold it for Canadian dollars on Quadriga to save a few bucks on transfer fees. Zou did it at the worst time, and he lost his life savings. He had planned to use the money for the down payment on an apartment.

As I read through the news of Gerry's death that afternoon and sat there in my apartment and digested the matter, the sun was already setting. Outside, a pink sheen lay upon the snow before it, too, receded.

In a moment incredulous and beyond imagination, I found myself in a situation that I didn't even know how I'd gotten into, or how I might ever find myself in again. It was midnight, and I was talking to a Russian on encrypted email, thirteen hours ahead of me, who allegedly had information that Gerald Cotten had faked his death and run off with all the users' money.

"Cotten's alive?" I asked.

"I have his new passport number, his home address, which he bought a long time ago in one of the CIS countries, and the address of the hotel he now lives." CIS stands for Commonwealth of Independent States, founded by twelve nations of the former Soviet Union, including Russia, Moldova, Belarus, and several countries ending with "stan." The Russian continued: "all materials exchange for money $ 50,000. I just do not write, I have these materials, and I know this and maybe a few more people, if you need information, then you have to agree with my conditions or just delete it all and go further."

"Any way you can prove your information's legit?"

The Russian ignored my question: "neither the law nor the court nor the stock exchange yet do not know about it."

"I get that." I pressed harder. "But any way you can show that you are who you are, and that you actually have the information you say you have?" It sounded in every way like a scam. "Anyone can say anything over the internet. Even in kidnappings, there's proof of life."

"I worry about my safety, he knows that I know everything about him," the Russian responded. "I can't tell you about myself." Indeed, I knew only two facts about that eastern European: the person had been using the free version of the Swiss-based encrypted-communications service ProtonMail, with Russian settings, and the person's time zone was in Omsk Oblast in southwestern Siberia, population under two million, bordering one former Soviet state, Kazakhstan.

Omsk is surprisingly similar to Calgary. Once Imperial Russia's southern frontier, it had sprouted out of a timber fort raised by steel-bearing Cossack riders in service of an expanding central government. Its flat plains thinly peopled, the town grew when the Trans-Siberian Railway came. Then Siberian oil. Omsk had known boom and bust. Yet its marshes and peat bogs — and, to the north, swampy forests — held a different memory, of fire and steel and revolution, from the monarchy to Communism to the collapse of the Soviet Union. Once hosting a prison camp to which the novelist Fyodor Dostoyevsky was exiled, the land bore trauma as if it had been printed by proud hooves in the receiving earth. It was an underdeveloped region whose per-capita GDP was below the national average. Omsk had tried to build a subway for more than twenty years. After billions of rubles, all it had to show were one station and a section of tracks. In 2012, the president went there to make promises, and the locals openly laughed.

The Russian continued about Gerry:

> as I heard, he planned this fraudulent scheme a few years ago, that moment there were people who recognized his scheme but no one knew when he would commit this scheme. Well, this information should know everything, I agree to the first payment of 50%, I will send you the materials, and you check, after checking you give me the remaining 50% of the amount, do you agree?

In Omsk that day, a light snowfall left little to no accumulation on the ground, its presence felt only in the soft southern breeze.

I didn't trust the Russian, and I did not respond.

With Gerry's death, mainstream attention on cryptocurrency shone white and hot again. Media across the world descended upon a courthouse in Halifax in eastern Canada for Quadriga's bankruptcy proceedings. That city was where Gerry and Jennifer had lived and where the man's funeral was held. It was a brutal introduction to Canada for many international journalists, for Halifax had a particularly harsh winter that year. Sometimes, the visibility was so poor, you could not even cross the street.

I ventured out of my Chinatown hovel to talk about Gerry on the radio for the Canadian Broadcasting Corporation (CBC). It was a Wednesday, and overhead was the cheerless gray, the snow dancing midair throughout the day. I sat in a studio by a table shaped in an elongated octagon, and around me were all sorts of fancy clocks, both digital and analog. I wore those huge headphones that people appearing on radio shows wear, the sort that feeds you back your voice as you speak — always an interesting experience. When hearing yourself speak normally, the sound vibrates through the skull, and your ears pick up a distorted version. When putting on those headphones, you hear the electronically transmitted words that, ironically, are as close you can ever get to hearing your own real voice. There is a reason many people find it uncomfortable to listen to recordings of themselves: it is jarring to have a long-held belief proven otherwise.

As I sat in the studio, ready to talk, there was a short pause in my world, suspended between one second and the next, as I reflected on the surrealness of it all. Months earlier, I had been holding Gerry's perforated steel–themed business card, white text on dark background, meaning to give him a call. I can't remember why I didn't end up dialing his Toronto number. Now I was going on the radio to talk about the fallout of his death.

"First of all," I said of Gerry, "I want to say my heart goes out to his widow and his family. He seemed like a nice guy."

Sometimes, I think back to that moment and marvel at how the first adjective I used publicly to describe Gerry was probably the most inaccurate one.

Throughout the ensuing year, investigations revealed that Gerry had moved users' money to personal accounts and had used part of it to gamble on risky cryptocurrency trades, including on the Dogecoin made in honor of the similarly named meme. Gerry was also accused of having used users' money to fund a lavish lifestyle, and of having created artificial trading volumes and inflating the company's revenue. As a teenager, Gerry had been allegedly scamming people by selling fraudulent get-rich-quick schemes on online forums. Jennifer eventually turned over the roughly $9 million she'd inherited from Gerry, saying she had been unaware of any wrongdoing.

But the most alarming news was something else. A *Vanity Fair* piece had an extra tidbit: police allegedly asked a witness "about twenty times" if Gerry was alive, saying "it's an open question." The doctor who treated him told the *Globe and Mail* newspaper the actual cause of death and its circumstances remained unclear. Then lawyers for Quadriga's creditors formally requested Canadian federal police to "conduct an exhumation and post-mortem autopsy on the body of Gerald Cotten to confirm both its identity and the cause of death given the questionable circumstances." A police spokesman declined to comment to media, as was procedure for an ongoing investigation, never saying whether the organization would or would not dig up the grave.

I eventually followed up with the Russian who had tried to sell me the alleged proof that Gerry did not die, but did not hear back. I started to doubt my skepticism. All that time, I had dismissed the notion as a conspiracy theory. I had even said so publicly during my interview with the CBC.

I was interviewed by Judy Aldous, a pixie-haired mother of three who had moved to Calgary from the far north, where she'd reported from trap lines and diamond mines. She had the sort of throaty yet smooth broadcaster voice I'd always envied. "Gerald Cotten is still alive living under an alias," she said, "and he stole all the Bitcoin — there's an endless number of conspiracy theories" — I laughed — "Are you buying any of this?"

"I do understand where the conspiracy theories are coming from," I said. "That guy laid out a will before he died with very specific instructions. He had instructions on how to care for his two dogs." Gerry had allocated $75,000 for the care of his chihuahuas. "It's quite inconceivable that if you have such a comprehensive will, you don't leave instructions on how to run your business." As well, India had a reputation for being a place where death certificates could be easily bought. But I also thought that betraying all who had trusted the exchange would have been just unimaginably vile. "I don't think he'll do us like this," I said of Gerry. "I would err on the side of giving the guy the benefit of the doubt."

"Yeah, and I think Foreign Affairs Canada has also said that someone died," Judy said. The government had issued a statement to that effect.

When I was done, I left the broadcaster's building and stepped without expectation into one of those frozen moments outside of time and space that you never forget. My lungs felt harsh and dry amid the winter air, the cursed flakes lingering unreasonably long, seemingly suspended as they floated from the leaden sky. People point at slush and say the crystals drift from the heavens pure, corrupted only by our mortal grime, but those of that view do not see there are bacteria in the snow. Born of plants, they rise to the atmosphere with the vapors and then mix with the clouds. When the flurries later melt upon the earth, or when it rains, the bacteria get ingested by the plants again. A cycle of dirt.

Beside the snow-covered streets, the Bow, just a little upriver from my apartment, was choppy, for a fast-moving waterway like that rarely freezes over. That felt disturbing in a way, almost going against nature, the current pushing against the shore as if angered, as if all its energy and its long journey — from the mountains' pale jagged peaks, white with the cold and often indistinguishable from the clouds, then through the gashes of their rocky faces, rushing east 80 miles as the buzzard flies — were going to culminate in something.

The following is extracted from the actual document. It has been selectively excerpted for length, but is otherwise unedited.

To the Royal Canadian Mounted Police:

Re: Quadriga CX – Request for Exhumation and Post-Mortem Autopsy of Gerald Cotten

The purpose of this letter is to request, on behalf of the Affected Users, that the Royal Canadian Mounted Police (the "**RCMP**"), conduct an exhumation and post-mortem autopsy on the body of Gerald Cotten to confirm both its identity and the cause of death given the questionable circumstances surrounding Mr. Cotten's death and the significant losses of Affected Users.

Enclosed please find a detailed compilation (the "**Background Material**," at Schedule "**A**") of publicly available information on the history of Quadriga, Gerald Cotten and others related to Quadriga which, in our view, further highlight the need for certainty around the question of whether Mr. Cotten is in fact deceased.

Representative Counsel respectfully requests that this process be completed by Spring of 2020, given decomposition concerns.

The Background Material has been created from publicly available information on the Quadriga matter.

Should the RCMP require anything further, Representative Counsel is available to assist.

Yours truly,

MILLER THOMSON LLP

Per:

[Signed]

Asim Iqbal
AIQ/

Encls.

CHAPTER 29

U nder the gray hue of the overcast sky, a showdown loomed. An icy gust blew from the north. A man entered Calgary's courthouse, a compound with an airy atrium: Dale Galbraith, who had sued Steve Carter's Oleum, heading for a pretrial conference. Two of the other lawsuits against Oleum had ended up settled. The third, by the printing company, succeeded when Oleum mounted no defense, but the plaintiff did not seem active in enforcing the judgment. Dale's suit was the only one outstanding, and that day in early 2019, after months of the man's having not seen Steve, that dispute was going to have its day.

Within Dale burned something strong. He had headed a grassroots association for the once-ruling Progressive Conservative party and had run in at least four elections at various levels. Dale had also served as a top staffer in an election campaign that the current mayor, back then a private citizen, had said was "noted for its bitterness and rancor." Long had Dale played among men who vied ruthlessly for the highest stakes. In his view, even though he was not someone who would start a confrontation, he would "give tit for tat." Dale was so confident, he was without a lawyer at that pretrial conference, going up alone against the Daves O'Connor and Bradley, Steve, and their legal counsel. Dale didn't need extra support for just that one meeting, he felt. He had 600 pages of documents. He was just as prepared as anyone else.

Something burned within Steve, too, as he walked into the courthouse, two tan towers of glass and metal that made up a "dignified contemporary facility," as described by the government. Oleum never listed on the Dutch Caribbean Securities Exchange as planned. It never listed anywhere, and it never sold any of its coins to the public as planned. Oleum's plans kept changing, and its dates kept getting pushed back. And Steve, whether justified or not, blamed Dale.

By itself, the project had already turned out to be a difficult one. Selling cryptocurrency to raise money had become a regulatory nightmare, precisely because of how easy initial coin offerings (ICO) had been. Everyone had been doing it, even the unsavory or incompetent. A *Wall Street Journal* investigation revealed one in five ICOs showed signs of fraud. A Boston College study found more than half of the projects died within four months of their ICOs. The social network Facebook banned ICO advertising. The U.S. Securities and Exchange Commission even created a website for a fake ICO to warn about fake ICOs, but that was the least of what it did. ICOs were touted as a way to raise money without going through the complex traditional route of an IPO (initial public offering), essentially bypassing the securities regulator. And the law did not like that. All over the world, regulators stepped in to claim jurisdiction, and they came for everyone. The action hero Steven Seagal ended up having to pay $314,000 to the SEC for his role in promoting something called "Bitcoiin2Gen." The boxer Floyd Mayweather and music producer DJ Khaled ended up settling with the SEC, too. One publication called celebrity endorsements of ICOs "a dumpster fire of epic proportions." China — a player so big, most of the world's Bitcoin was at one point traded in the country's yuan currency — banned ICOs altogether.

Against that backdrop, Oleum did not have an easy time. "Trying to do it all to the letter of the law slowed everything down," the co-founder Dave Bradley told me. "We eventually stopped pushing." Then time ground on Oleum. By 2019, the ICO craze had died. According to one report, projects would raise just $371 million that year, compared to almost $8 billion in 2018. Oleum's $200 million target now looked comically ambitious. "We probably would have a hard time filling the sale," Dave said. "That's the reward for doing everything by the book."

To Steve, the dispute with Dale had been a significant diversion of energy and resources: "We spent two months just dealing with his stuff, basically, constant noise and whatnot." Because of that, Oleum ended up missing the period during which investors were wild about ICOs, Steve said, adding that the dispute had "cost us time, number one, which in crypto space is like gold."

Pretrial conferences are called "informal," yet they are anything but. Before Steve and Dale met, the court would have prepared for them a long list of dos and don'ts, with an entire section on etiquette that included instructions like "Speak calmly and clearly; do not interrupt others," and "Address the Judge as 'Your Honour,' Legal Counsel as 'Mr. ___' or 'Ms. ___' and the Court Clerk as 'Master Clerk' or 'Madam Clerk.'" For the Oleum pretrial, records show it was even held in a courtroom. The only true informality of such conferences is they are "without prejudice," meaning nothing anyone says can be used against them if the case goes to trial. Such conferences are meant to help parties reach settlement to avoid an expensive and exhausting open-court confrontation. "Do not bring any witnesses," read the list of dos and don'ts. At a pretrial conference, people need to be able to speak frankly and freely.

And that they did.

"I'm no stranger to confrontation," Dale described himself to me. "I don't mind it. I can handle myself in any situation." By his recollection, he was hard and restless at the pretrial conference, hammering Steve on the financial situation of the legal entities associated with the company. "Is there money in Oleum Capital Inc.?" Dale pressed. "Is there money in Oleum Capital Holdings Inc.?"

According to Dale, Steve responded each time: "No, there's no money in Oleum Capital Inc." "No, there's no money in Oleum Capital Holdings Inc."

It is important to note that, in keeping with their purpose, pretrial conferences are not open to the public, neither are they usually recorded by the court, and nor is any participant allowed to tape them. To me, Steve did not dispute Dale's account of his line of questioning, but he added context: the company was not broke. It's just that everything had been allocated. There was no spare money. But beyond the initial exchange, there is little agreement as to what happened.

What is undisputed, though, is the strong emotion that ran through that meeting. At the end of the pretrial conference, held on the eighth floor of the judicial complex, the only resolution was to move the case to a higher court. Nothing was settled that day, nor any day since.

But given the sorry state of Oleum, nothing mattered. Even just logistically, the company would shrivel, vacating its shiny BP oil office in the middle of downtown to go without a physical location. Steve would tell me the company was planning to rent space in a WeWork communal office. Oleum would also be late in filing its legally required annual paperwork — more than a year after its due date. It was a reflection of the sort of purgatory the company was in, waiting for regulatory developments, waiting for the markets — incomplete, unfulfilled, like that pretrial conference. Dave Bradley would tell me he still believed in the concept behind Oleum, but added: "Nobody is running it per se. . . . If you bring it back, I don't know, I don't know if everybody will still be involved in it again." Since co-founding Oleum, Dave had started a new Bitcoin brokerage, and he was focused on that. Dave even removed Oleum from his LinkedIn page. He was a man knowledgeable in the way the wind blew.

For Steve, all of that must have been painfully disappointing. Oleum was not just Steve's idea. It had been his entrance into the new world of crypto-blockchain. He was no Bitcoin forefather of the city like Dave, who seemingly had a hand in everything, and Steve was invested in Oleum on a much deeper level. Oleum was Steve's baby — his only baby. It was also something else. As I looked into the company, I would learn that everything I thought I knew about Steve was only surface-level. There was a lot about his past that I had not known. Oleum had been the potential key to breaking a longstanding pattern in Steve's life, the one big haul that could have changed it all.

CHAPTER 30

B orn in 1981, on the anniversary of the first Grey Cup foot-
ball game, Stephen Paul Carter lived frugally as a young man,
his monthly expenditures being just $130 for food and $22 for
clothing. There was nothing for alcohol or dining out, Steve's one
creature comfort being $36 per month for cigarettes, an utterly
moderate expense not meant for any serious smoker. Steve was
not a man of excess, for he didn't have the means. Steve had
worked for a security company for a year and a half, but he did
not get paid as promised. So he took out a loan and used credit
cards before falling behind on payments, becoming, in his words,
"unable to catch up." In 2006, Steve's 1996 Volkswagen Golf was
seized by his landlord at the service shop, towed to the impound
lot, and sold at a public auction. That year, younger than I was
when I left university, Steve became bankrupt. He owed some
$26,000, the bulk of it to banks but also more than $100 to the
Blockbuster Video rental chain.

Two years later, Steve saw the opportunity for profit in the
2008 financial crisis, forming a plan to invest in American real
estate, but he knew little of what he was doing. The plan spiraled
out of control and failed. Then, toward the end of that year, Steve
was in a nondescript suburban community experiencing one of
the worst nights of his life.

Across the land, the river Bow snaked for close to 400 miles, the icy rush between snow-covered banks. It flowed east until it reached the site of the Mountie outpost that spawned the city. Just a little after that, the river took a hard right, flowing south, down and down. Along the waterflow went the law. Three days before the Christmas of 2008, a special task force raided the house Steve was in — 40 Heritage Lake Mews contained a cache of guns, pipe bombs, and drugs. With Steve were two local gangsters: Real Honorio, who ten days later killed someone, and Anthony Beare, an easterner who sometimes used cocaine, described by a psychological assessment as "impulsive" and "influenced by magical thinking." Also present was Beare's common-law wife and a mysterious man of whom little is publicly known other than the name Sopha Moeun. The hapless, then-27-year-old Steve was, in his words, "not at all in any way, shape, or form involved with them," although he declined to elaborate out of what he said was concern for his safety. "I was definitely the victim in that situation," Steve said of his presence in the house. "I was forcibly there." It was a bittersweet moment as police stormed the house that night. "Wrong place, wrong time," in his view, Steve was arrested for doing no wrong, yet all that ran through his head was a gladness "that somebody was there." While nobody was ever charged with forcible confinement, the law does somewhat back up Steve's account that he was not involved — he, along with Sopha Moeun, faced no charges. And I believe him. Yet whether or not Steve knew it at the time, his life was about to take a turn.

The American real-estate venture from earlier that year came back to bite Steve. He might have had good intentions, but he had found the wrong partner, and the venture had involved too many people, taken too much money. The police started investigating. In 2013, Steve was convicted of fraud. Then he was sued for more than $7 million in a separate investment scheme. Much of that was claimed as interest, which Steve did not believe he owed, but it was a difficult time. He was going through a lot. Against that suit, Steve did not put up a fight, and the court ruled against him in default.

In the wake of that, Steve set his eyes on entrepreneurship again. He wanted to start a successful company. Steve did not know if he had always made the right decisions. But he wanted to rebuild, to change for the better, as if all the bludgeonings of life had given him something strong.

Steve went on to start the Luxx Group, a luxury-lifestyle membership service. There was some overlap between that and Oleum. Dale Galbraith said Steve tried to get him to invest in Luxx. The website said it would launch in 2018. Steve said it never launched. But Luxx did get sued a fair bit. There was a lawsuit from a custom-home builder for about $65,000, another from a law firm for an unspecified amount, and yet another from a marketing firm for some $20,000. While the former two appear unresolved, court records show the last was settled when Dave O'Connor agreed to pay the amount via installments. As Steve made his way to the courthouse for the pretrial conference with Dale, he must have felt a sort of dark déjà vu — and not just about Luxx.

That judicial complex was touted as the biggest in the country and housed different courts that were once in separate facilities. Steve had been returning to that place far more than anyone would want to. In his mind, "nobody likes going to court" — "it's just not some place to be." Steve was gearing for a big new fight, in a new world where he had made a new life, but the past was all around him.

For more than a year, Steve had had a fancy downtown office and worn fancy suits and had the sort of respect in the local scene that many in his past had denied him. Crypto-blockchain, that new world, could have represented a fresh beginning for Steve, like it had for so many others. "I think life is what it is, and you have to take it with what you can, and go from there and move on from there," Steve said, when I asked whether he thought fortune was fair. "Yeah, I don't really know. I wouldn't say whether it was fair or unfair." It was a hard question to answer, he said. "It's been tough. You know, it's — it's been one thing after another, for sure."

Steve remained optimistic about Oleum, far more so than the co-founder Dave Bradley. "If we were to take a company public, a three-to-four-year time frame — typically you go public within five years — so, we look at it as that kind of a play now," Steve told me. "I hope to look back in four years and be like, 'Look what we did. It took us longer, but we're here.'" But soon, Oleum's website went down, and the company got struck off the corporate registry for not filing its annual paperwork. I never heard about Oleum again. If Steve had been searching for something within cryptocurrency, I don't think he ever found it.

Some others on this frontier, though, appeared to have more luck.

CHAPTER 31

As the probe by the Alberta Securities Commission continued, Jan Cerato returned from Mexico rested and recharged. He had earlier proposed to the investigator Louise Panneton a date in early 2019 for a meeting, and he felt confident and prepared as he took on the commission. "When i went head to head with them in the room," Jan told me much later in a text message, when I approached him about this book, "they were so shook up they couldnt write with their pens or communicate properly constantly pausing for breaks, half way through they knew that i was clean clear and not involved in anything they thought i was!" Jan said of Louise: "I didnt let them pin any of their false fake bullshit on me and she worked for over a year on that file! She quit moved back to ontario! My lawyer crushed all if [sic] their false evidence and assumtions [sic]!"

I've not been able to verify Jan's account of how the meeting went, but his information on Louise's move is mostly accurate. Soon after the meeting that Jan described, according to records I've obtained via a freedom-of-information request, Louise was in the east, picking up a fresh BlackBerry phone and a new investigator's badge, and attending "Cybersecurity Awareness Training." Louise was in Gatineau, Quebec, just across the river from Canada's capital of Ottawa, in the sixteen-floor downtown building of the federal body that oversees elections, a mish-mash of curves and angles and glass and concrete sitting at the French-language address 30 Rue Victoria. The lead investigator on Jan's case had indeed left the commission.

Like Louise's motivation for moving west in the first place, her specific reason for going back east is mysterious to me. But it was no surprise. Louise's email auto-response at the elections organization began French first, *"Je serai absente du bureau . . ."* The ensuing English portion was riddled with stylistic incon-sistencies, using both "email" and "e-mail" and missing a comma when listing years after dates. While that may not seem like a big deal to little ol' you and me, linguistic precision is serious business for lawyers like Louise, who sometimes spar mercilessly over the smallest details — in 2018, a dairy company in Portland, Maine, lost $5 million because of a missing comma. Indeed, the French portion of Louise's auto-response was flawless, and her imper-fections in English involved only those nuances that did not exist in her mother tongue. That aspect of Louise's writing shows not just something in itself but an element of a larger pattern. Even at the commission, all the way across the land, Louise still had a Google alert for her former employer, the Autorité des marchés financiers, Quebec's securities regulator, and she'd set it to ping more frequently than some of her other such setups. Louise might have left Quebec, but Quebec had never left her. The West, with all its eccentricities, was never truly home.

And then there was silence, publicly at least, from the commission. For those outside, it was unclear where the investi-gation was heading. In the wake of that, Jan started promoting a questionable investment: Cloud Wallet, or Cloud Token as it was also sometimes called. Originating in Malaysia, Cloud purportedly used artificial intelligence to trade cryptocurrency on behalf of users, with up to 15 percent monthly returns.

At one Thursday meetup at the casino, Jan explained how, in his view, the product worked. "The Cloud Token company takes all the Bitcoin and the Ethereum from all of us" — he pointed at the meetup audience, his index fingers circling — "and they put it into that 1.5 billy right there on Binance." Jan moved to point at the screen. Binance, known as the world's largest exchange, had at the time $1.5 billion in trade volume daily. "There's no bullshit about this." He pointed to the computer screen with all five fingers. "Our money's right at the top of the food chain." It had not taken long for Jan to use plural pronouns when referring to Cloud, which he called his "favorite little baby." At one point, Jan started calling himself "the CEO of CTOGlobal.io Company which is the North & South American distributor of the App brand from Asia called Cloud 2.0."

Cloud users received bonuses if they persuaded others to sign up through them, much like iPro Network, the project whose earlier event listed Jan as the organizer, with which he later denied any association. In his first Facebook post about Cloud, Jan targeted "Friends that need more money." He later wrote about all the success he said he was having, saying in one of his posts that he was making "clean money."

Cryptocurrency scams would rake in $4.3 billion in 2019, more than triple 2018's haul, according to the blockchain intelligence firm Chainalysis. Ninety-two percent of them would be the so-called Ponzi schemes. As much as they are devastating to most participants, they are also profitable for those who get in early, when later investors' money is used to pay purported returns to prior ones to maintain the veil of legitimacy. You just need to know it is unsustainable, and to cash out while you still can. Some, in fact, made a lot of money from the infamous Bitconnect, getting to the chest of gold before the ship sank to the seabed.

At the Thursday meetup, while Jan did not outright promote Cloud and had a disclaimer that he was not providing investment advice, he addressed the criticism Cloud had attracted. "It's never a Ponzi till it's over." Jan held out his palm and pointed at one of his fingers, as if he was about to rattle off a list. "It's only a Ponzi when it's over, so keep that in mind." Jan repeated his point as he curled his fingers before expanding them, almost mimicking an explosion. "Do your homework and find out what's really cooking before you throw your dough in."

Jan bounced a little on his feet, open palms up and down, edgewise toward the ground like a rapper. "People are still shitting on me because of Cloud Token, because they don't get it." In the past, Jan had praised Bitconnect and two other collapsed investment schemes. Jan continued, "I'm like, 'Buddy, I'm out there making dough.'" Cloud had been accused of being mysterious and offering little information about itself, but that did not matter. "What do you need to know?'" Jan shrugged slightly. "You need to know who the owner is to make money?" He smacked a fist on a palm twice in quick succession. "You need to know where the office is located to make money? Do you care? Do you care if they registered their website on GoDaddy or not" — Jan waved a palm in front of his face — "to hide their info or something? I don't care about any of that. I see people get so petty about all these little details, and none of that stuff pays the bills."

Some lickspittle sycophant at the back laughed loudly every time he thought Jan said something clever, his joy spewing from what I would imagine to be a yawning chasm of a mouth, rows of animal-like little teeth tightly packed together.

Jan eventually made it all the way to Kuala Lumpur, Malaysia's capital, for a Cloud event, emerging out of a helicopter in white sunglasses and the same colorful shirt in which he was photographed at the iPro event of 2017. Jan made a video he shared on social media, in which he said: "These haters, and all these people that are saying, 'You can't do this, Jan, you can't do that, who do you think you are?'" — he shook his head — "Where are they now?"

ACT VI

2019 HIGH: $13,800

CHAPTER 32

I spent the deepest part of winter between 2018 and 2019 in Toronto, much of it hanging out with the now-former Oleum contractor Elias Ahonen, who had by then become a friend, duing a period that may or may not have involved psychedelics. His friend Kieran Macleod, also of the cryptocurrency world, joined us this one time. Kieran was a vegetarian and healthier than both Elias and I put together, and that day was the first time in my life I tasted kombucha, the gassy fermented tea. The three of us would later share a connection. Kieran would join Elias and me in having spent time at the wild cryptocurrency incubator on the Thai island, with the swimming pool shaped like genitalia. Before then, that period in Toronto was dreamlike, phantasmagorical.

Somehow, throughout the great cryptocurrency winter, I had narrowly escaped being mounted on the wall, credit due largely to my business partner, Winsor Hoang, and partly to luck, in a story that always made me feel weird when I told it. I was in clover, and my field ran deep.

The way a Bitcoin mining company operates is that profitability depends on cheap power. If it spends less on electricity to make one bitcoin than its market price, it profits. Late 2018, Bitcoin was falling so much, running the mining machines was costing many companies more than the value of the resulting cryptocurrency. So Winsor had a proposition for our power provider: If the company were to collapse, there would be nobody to buy the electricity, and nobody would make money. Why not give us a lower electricity rate so all would continue to profit? We ended up with a one-quarter reduction, and that gave us a handsome profit margin even in the downturn. We got a bailout, like those received by the banks ten years earlier. Our problem was solved by the same greed and lack of accountability that sparked our entire industry. The irony of that did not escape me. It was so thick, you could stuff a mattress with it, and I kept thinking about it. Sometimes you think you're the chimp that saw the first fire, you think you're Marco Polo, but then you realize you're just a tourist, with legions before you and legions after, gawking at the Great Wall.

Mid-2019, Bitcoin rose back to the five digits, briefly reaching a high of nearly $14,000. It reflected broader growth, beyond price. Companies and governments were seemingly following Facebook in planning for its own digital currency, with many hiring blockchain talent. Those efforts were far from Bitcoin, or even actual cryptocurrency sometimes, but they were not meaningless. There was an energy returning to the sector, buoyed by Ethereum again. The decentralized applications on it and similar platforms, called dApps, which run without central administrators, were blossoming in all sorts of direc-tions. The hottest one at the time was decentralized finance, or DeFi, banking and investing on effectively self-running systems. Big investors, the whales, were also buying up more bitcoins. It was sunrise after a night of storm, the dewy fields sparkling in the dawn. The downturn had been harsh, and I was no longer a millionaire, but I had risen back to a comfortable level. I probably had as much money as a moderately successful but unremarkable lawyer of my age, and I no longer wanted anything more.

I was tired.

Time moves faster in the cryptocurrency world. When I was at Reuters writing about the international oil markets, a 5 percent move in price was a big deal for which we had to immediately send an alert. Once, a 5 percent fall for an oil company's stock elicited a frantic call from my editor, heart in throat: "Ethan, what's going on?" For Bitcoin, that's Tuesday, and not even the whole Tuesday. Just Tuesday morning. Among Bitcoin's biggest single-day moves was an almost 40 percent surge, made in 2017. This is a world in which decades truly happen within weeks. Events can end quickly, just as quickly as people spit in their hands and shake them, like the short-lived mayfly, experiencing all the trials and triumphs of life in just one day, sired at sunrise, dead at dusk.

And in a field built on a volatile asset class, one's survival hinges, more than anything else, on the dominance of the logical mind over irrational emotion. Even if talking about just the traditional markets, the black-clad hedge-fund psychologist in the television series *Billions* says: "An average trader makes a trade and feels good. A great trader makes a trade and feels" — she scrunches up her nose and raises her voice — "nothing." If you act out of panic or overconfidence, it will almost certainly be the wrong move. But that is also the most instinctual and natural thing. Television does not romanticize how draining it is to suppress one's impulses and to maintain that. I want to say I felt like those clone troopers in the Star Wars franchise, who age at twice the rate of ordinary humans, but that would be an understatement. What I truly felt was as if I had gone to sleep one night and then woken up chain-smoking and scowling like some world-weary aging actor, perhaps Clint Eastwood.

I cared less and less about the company. While I still had my personal cryptocurrency investments and my stake in the business, I increasingly left most of the day-to-day operations to my long-suffering business partner, Winsor. I still held my meetups, but it had long since devolved into just a Wednesday night at the pub with my buddies. At the same time, I had gotten a visitorship at the University of British Columbia, and separately, I made the arrangements for this book and started to write it. In cryptocurrency, I felt I was like the author Bill Bryson when he wanders the United Kingdom in *Notes from a Small Island*: "I couldn't say where I went exactly because Manchester's streets always seem curiously indistinguishable to me. I never felt as if I were getting nearer to or farther away from anything in particular but just wandering around in a kind of urban limbo." Much of 2019 marked a sort of purgatorial phase for me, a period of reflection, pondering the paths behind and before me, like a butterfly crawling back into the cocoon. I can't say I found any answers, but I did arrive at an action. I had often thought back to when it all began, before I bought any Bitcoin, before moving west to Calgary, in that little seaside town where the spoiled milk in the trash bins smelled like cheese, when I had that phone call with Anthony Di Iorio in which he called Bitcoin a game changer. It seemed so distant and foreign, as if that conversation had been had by two other men, speaking French or some other language of which I knew little. I had to see the Ethereum co-founder again.

CHAPTER 33

I t was only a little bit surprising when I watched Anthony Di
Iorio announce his retirement on stage at a Toronto cryptocurrency conference, held at a waterfront nightclub. It was
August 2019, and Anthony was turning to philanthropy, motivated by the demands of modern living, the feeling of being
overwhelmed by constant connection, which he had both felt
himself and wanted to alleviate in others. Retirement may seem
early for a man not even 45 years old. But in cryptocurrency,
someone like Anthony, who entered in 2012, might as well be an
elder statesman. Anthony's motivation was not directly related
to cryptocurrency, but that is a world that amplifies everything, a
rough realm where everything tends to the extremes and where
nothing is small nor simple.

Even on the day of Anthony's announcement, when he
gave his keynote address on a stage with a galaxy background,
where the lights bathed everything in blue, his motivation rang
true. There seemed to be so many things pulling and tugging at
him in every direction.

At the bar area, amid all the hugs and the cryptocurrency
enthusiasts seeking selfies — "I'm the biggest fan!" said one
woman — as I stood talking to him, Anthony discovered he was
missing his phone, whose lockscreen was his girlfriend's picture.

He went back to the stage to search for it. Then as we walked to Anthony's car — a long walk through the lakeside breeze, for he had come late and thus had to park far away — phone back in pocket, a half dozen or so members of his entourage in tow, he wondered, "Wait a second, where're my keys?"

"Keys?"

They were found quickly, within five seconds. "There you go."

"Ah! All right!"

"We're good. We're good. Let's do it."

"Phone, keys — we gotta get you a fanny pack."

There was little attention for me as well. I had wanted to talk at the conference, but Anthony had little time — although he was kind enough to give me a ride — and I had to schedule a phone call, which we were able to make happen only two months later. Anthony didn't even attend the conference. He came for his talk, he stayed for an hour, and off he went in his luxury SUV, with the creamy white leather interior and a small but firm pillow on each seat. That evening, Anthony was planning a surprise birthday party for a friend. Then there was a funeral the next day. A friend's fourteen-year-old nephew had taken his own life, Anthony said. "I'm spending the full day tomorrow going through these things." There was no doubt a lot on Anthony's mind that day, though perhaps no more than any other day.

A billionaire's attention is a precious, precious commodity. There was little to no fiction in Anthony's library. Instead he read practical books like *How to Be a Chief Operating Officer* and *Key Performance Indicators* and deep dives into companies such as Apple and Toyota, and he had an unusually high number of Patrick Lencioni business-management tomes. He wore a work uniform of only T-shirts, jeans, and sneakers to cut down on decision-making, owning so few items of clothing that everything fit in a small corner of his walk-in closet (it's not so much *his* closet as his girlfriend's). In fact, so focused on efficiency was Anthony, that was why he'd left the project for which he was best known. He had disagreed with the move to form the Ethereum Foundation to support the platform, instead of a for-profit company. "We don't want to be the Mozilla of this," he told an interviewer. "We want to be the Google of crypto."

W e snaked through Toronto's gridlock, Anthony and I and his girlfriend, Maggie Xu. Driving the car was Anthony's elder brother, Elio, not yet 50, graying, a former municipal politician. Electronic music blared, synthesized beats filling the car as it mounted the highway — Above & Beyond, a British trio formed in 2000. "This is live from Wembley," Anthony said of the performance, recorded at the London indoor arena in 2015. Anthony liked what he called its energy, joy, and "representation of love." He asked for the music to be turned up. Anthony hummed along.

"We've been doing a lot of Above & Beyond," Maggie said. There was an almost constant skin-to-skin contact between her and Anthony, even as she sat up front and he behind. Maggie, a lawyer by training, was to be Anthony's successor, taking over Decentral. An ethnic Chinese woman who, in her words, "grew up in a very traditional family," Maggie was almost Anthony's opposite. Unlike her boyfriend, who did what he liked and coasted through university for his marketing degree, Maggie's post-secondary life was "eight-hour classes, and then we start going to the library for another four." That part of her remained, even as she moved into the new world of blockchain. As "We're All We Need" rang through the car, Maggie casually said she had been asked to moderate a law panel the next day.

I couldn't help but receive that news with mild amusement. It was the sort of public-speaking heads-up the free-wheeling

Anthony did not give when he called Maggie up on stage during his earlier keynote.

"I had no idea, okay," Maggie said to her boyfriend, only half in jest. "My hands were shaking."

"You have to know everything, don't you?" Anthony teased. "You have to know everything."

"Well, yeah, when you're being invited on stage to give a speech."

Anthony later told me, "I like surprises." He had done the same to his brother, Elio.

Anthony's Decentral, on which he focused after leaving the Ethereum project, was perhaps best known for the Jaxx multi-cryptocurrency wallet, whose main source of profit was at one point an integration with the exchange platform ShapeShift, which facilitated anonymous trades. When Jaxx users swapped one coin for another through ShapeShift, part of the related transaction fee went to Decentral, and at its highest that amounted to $300,000 a month. But that fell when ShapeShift started needing personal information from customers. And, of course, the markets had dropped, in a bitter winter that had come without discrimination, its snow thickly drifted, formless and formlessly falling on all the rich and the poor alike. Decentral laid off nearly half of its workers, down to fourteen. The offices were shuttered. Even Anthony himself had been affected. While it was partly because his $21 million condominium had good security, it was also because he had become less wealthy, and his "risk profile" had changed — he got rid of the bodyguards he had had for a while. That day in the car, Anthony was a lot less imposing than when I'd seen him last, speaking at the conference the previous year with muscled guys in tow. I saw Anthony bearded for the first time, his face peppered with the sort of gray I never knew he had.

For all I know, Anthony had just neglected shaving for a couple of days, but I like to think the universe had imbued a deeper meaning into his facial hair, for I'm a guy who likes to read too much into things. In the world of television, "Growing the Beard" is a trope that references a "definitive moment when a series begins to become noticeably better in quality," a term popularized after *Star Trek*'s improvement coincided with Commander Riker's sporting facial hair. To be whiskered is also, somehow, a time-honored practice for clean-shaven American men who step back from prominent roles: the late basketballer Kobe Bryant; celebrities David Letterman, Jim Carrey, and Jon Stewart; and politicians Ted Cruz and Beto O'Rourke — the list goes on. But it's not solely a so-called retirement beard; it's also dubbed the metamorphosis beard. Men grow it when they embark on new projects. A *Washington Post* writer quipped that the American politician Al Gore's beard in the early 2000s said "in whiskers instead of words: 'I don't give a damn. I am reborn.'"

After Decentral endured the cryptocurrency winter, the company started growing and hiring again, with an ambitious new Jaxx and a vision of expansion under Maggie, the new chief executive. Anthony remained chairman, and he would continue to fund the company, depending on what Maggie wanted to do, but he set his sights elsewhere. Philanthropy was a plan formed, in part, after meeting the Hollywood actor Leonardo DiCaprio, Anthony said, who had a charitable foundation under his name. The two had a loose connection: Anthony had been an advisor to a blockchain project that involved a DiCaprio-produced movie, and had gone to the actor's house.

On the day of the Toronto conference, what had been kept close to the vest had been unburdened unto the world. Sitting behind Maggie, Anthony had a palm on his girlfriend's shoulder, on which she put hers sometimes. Sometimes he kissed her hand. Every now and then, Anthony gave directions to his brother, Elio, who steered the car northwest, away from the waterfront. Anthony called up his friend Oliver to invite him to that night's surprise birthday party. He noticed Fat Bastard Burrito had changed its logo. He talked about his travel plans to Miami and Costa Rica. Beyond talking about the conference the next day, there was not a whisper of Bitcoin or blockchain.

I thought a lot about Anthony afterward, and when I slept that night, it was deep and dreamless.

CHAPTER 34

The next day of the Toronto conference ended with a pool party, and Anthony was not there. I sat by the water, a Corona beer in hand from the open bar, a burger in my belly from the gourmet buffet, an inflatable swan in the pond before me. The pool aspect of the party seemed poorly advertised, and only one person, a friend whom I knew from Calgary, had brought her swimsuit, although there was this jackass who jumped into the water in all his clothes. The air smelled of barbecue and sweat, and of summer.

I doubt Anthony will long remember me, but meeting him after all those years — after everything — and learning of his retirement had given me a clarity and a calm that was hard to describe. I felt empty, but not the bad kind of empty. I was empty of thirst, empty of want, empty of joy, but also empty of troubles. That day, an overwhelming brightness hung on the pool — the figurative but also the literal, for all the service staff were in white, like guests at one of those fancy French Dîner en Blanc events. The moment felt pleasing, like seeing your pinwheel catch the wind, or the first cut with a pair of scissors into a fresh piece of construction paper. The days were still long, and it was as if the sunset would never come.

But the season was ending and so was the party.

At the pool, I ran into people from the rambunctious Thai island to which I'd gone earlier. I was not expecting to see them, but there they were, and I was happy to see them. I wondered if I should take psychedelics, like all my islander friends who had smuggled it over. The big boss from the island who funded the incubator was there, too, and he seemed to be on something all the time, although for such a big man, he was really stealthy, and I'd caught only a glimpse of him and not his eye. I switched to drinking gin and tonics — four or five of them, I cannot remember. What I can never forget, though, was seeing Kieran Macleod in a wheelchair.

Kieran had broken his back in Thailand, when he went to the same island where I had been and met the same people. Kieran had had a motorcycle accident — "titanium plates to his back, stitches to a wound on his head, and wraps to cover various road-rash injuries on his body," so read an online fundraising page. That in itself was not news to me, but it was the first time I had seen Kieran since we last met, pre-accident, and it was jarring. Through no fault of his own, the man could no longer walk. Mentally, I had always associated my time on the island with carefreeness, warmth, and unbridled joy. It could easily have been me in that wheelchair. That day, I remembered the taste of the island wind, the smell of the sea, and never again so remembered them.

I never did end up partaking in the islanders' drugs, for I had meetings the next day. Then the open bar ended. Surprisingly, it lasted only about an hour, compared to two the previous year. Maybe the open bar wasn't based on a time limit, but the number of drinks sold, and we simply drank faster in 2019. But it was also only one night of free drinks, compared to two, and the food, good as it was, felt noticeably cheaper. Somehow, there were few of us who noticed, and so many new faces at the conference, so many who came because Bitcoin was booming again, so many that did not even know there was a limit to the open bar.

Sitting by the water, I was increasingly not in a particularly pool-party mood. I was acutely aware that, though I had enjoyed myself at the conference the year before — this being the very conference at which the late Larry King spoke — I was now a different man in a different time. Around me were people I knew and revelry that beckoned me, but somehow I felt alone, like a man marooned. Then dusk came. In the water, the blow-up bird bobbed amid the waning sun, and shadows grew upon the swan. I did not know at the time that the Ethereum that Anthony had co-founded was going to be in the news for the most unexpected of reasons, and it had a connection to me that would shake me to my core.

CHAPTER 35

It was Thanksgiving of 2019. Ethereum's Virgil Griffith was planning to fly from Los Angeles to Baltimore to be with his parents, sister, and her family, but he never made it. At the airport that morning, under the dull and steely sky, Virgil got arrested.

Handcuffs are heavy, and there's a weight on the wrists, particularly on the little bumpy bone on the end of the forearm. The edges of the cuffs are square, so they dig in, even when they are loose. If you struggle, you bruise and erode the skin. Without the ability to swing the arms, it's also hard to maintain balance when walking, and if you fall with hands behind your back, you crash directly on your face. To be in irons would certainly not be a familiar feeling for Virgil, who had never before been in significant trouble with the law. But the thoughts within him likely hurt more than any physical discomfort: the answer to the question of why.

It was no riddle at all per se. After all, the Federal Bureau of Investigation (FBI) had been in touch just two weeks earlier. But the fact that "why" had to be asked, the fact the arrest was happening at all, was definitely painful.

Ethereum was anticipating a "hard fork" the following week, a sort of network upgrade whose successful implementation depended on consensus within the leaderless, horizontally structured blockchain system. The team had worked hard on it for a long time. But the weight of the task never marred Ethereum's trademark whimsicality, often distilled in the public's eye in the co-founder Vitalik Buterin's wearing of rainbow and unicorn T-shirts, even among straitlaced, suited company. The hard fork was dubbed "Istanbul," coming after another network upgrade, "Constantinople," the older name for the Turkish city — those with an eye for this will see references to pop culture, history, and game theory all rolled into one. As head of special projects at the Ethereum Foundation, Virgil may or may not have worked directly on the upgrade, but to someone like him, who once suspended his doctoral studies to participate in the reality television series *King of the Nerds*, the whole Ethereum brand and the names of the forks must have all been very neat and clever, worthy of a nice chuckle every time it came to mind. Virgil's conversation two weeks earlier with the FBI — an organization that, according to a friend, had at one point left him "convinced they totally got where he was coming from" — was probably the last thing he wanted to think about.

But think about it, he had to. At the airport, Virgil was being arrested for his alleged part in a "conspiracy" at the North Korean conference that I'd attended, accused of trying to give the country "technical advice on using cryptocurrency and blockchain technology to evade sanctions." Virgil faced up to twenty years in prison.

The Telegram chat group we had for the North Korea trip, dormant for months, with only a handful still posting, suddenly buzzed with activity.

Another high-profile cryptocurrency arrest had also happened at an airport, that of the proverbial "first felon" Charlie Shrem, the earliest cryptocurrency-linked person to be convicted in a major case.

A New Yorker, Shrem had founded BitInstant, a brokerage where Bitcoin could be bought using dollars, back when such platforms were still rare. It was a big deal, at one point accounting for almost 30 percent of all Bitcoin transactions. BitInstant was also backed by the Winklevoss twins. But despite rising to become a celebrity-like figure in Bitcoin, Shrem reportedly cared little for the corporate side of things and eventually ran afoul of money-laundering laws.

On a trip home from Amsterdam in 2014, Shrem was talking anthropology with his girlfriend — musing about liminality, a sort of disorientation people experience in the purgatorial middle stage of rites of passage, and how that was analogous to an airport — when men in uniforms approached, took him by the arm, and led him, amid the stares of the crowd, to a room in the back before hauling him away in a caravan of black SUVs.

Beyond the airport arrest, another similarity between Shrem's and Virgil's cases is that both involved the same division of the justice department: the United States Attorney's Office for the Southern District of New York. While it is no different from any other district in name, it oversees the country's financial and cultural center, meaning that, in practice, it is in a class of its own. That office is even better for the résumé than the elite law schools, high-powered firms, and eminent clerkships from which it draws its ranks, according to the *New York Times*, which called it "one of the city's most powerful clubs." That is also the office that prosecuted another high-profile Bitcoin case, that of Ross Ulbricht, a Texan who ran the dark web market website Silk Road, on which weapons and drugs were sold. That office had pursued Jeffrey Epstein, the highly connected billionaire sex offender; U.S. president Donald Trump's fixer and lawyer Michael Cohen; Bernie Madoff, proponent of the largest Ponzi scam in history; and mafia headmen of New York's "Five Families." When Trump became president, and his administration asked all appointees by his predecessor to step down, the then-head of the Southern District, Preet Bharara — who, incidentally, had announced the charges of both the Bitcoiners Shrem and Ulbricht — defiantly said no. Bharara was fired, but that did not stop the district from looking into the president's inauguration committee. So notable the Southern District is, it inspired an entire television show, *Billions*, with a key character modeled after Bharara. There was no question that, out of the tall grass, something dangerous had come for Virgil.

The head of the Southern District, Geoffrey Berman, said in a statement Virgil had "jeopardized" the government's sanctions. Berman's boss, John Demers, said the justice department wanted to "begin the process of seeking justice for such conduct." A senior FBI man, William Sweeney, said, "We cannot allow anyone to evade sanctions. . . . It's even more egregious that a U.S. citizen allegedly chose to aid our adversary."

As what remained of the Pyongyang eight discussed the news in our Telegram group, a question ran through our minds: how had this happened? Parts of the allegations related to matters only we knew.

CHAPTER 36

The answer was anticlimactic. It was all Virgil. He had talked to the authorities willingly and told them everything, the bureau said. If you read the official complaint from the justice department, it was actually all quite baffling. It was as if Virgil was trying to descend from the second story of a house but had managed to somehow fall up the stairs.

Americans are a special breed. They are taxed on their worldwide income, even if they live outside the country, and they are not allowed to go to North Korea without express permission, after the case of Otto Warmbier, the young American from Cincinnati, Ohio, who died after being detained in the totalitarian state. So like any good U.S. citizen, Virgil had sought said permission from the Department of State, according to the official complaint, a legal document from the justice department. In it, an FBI special agent said Virgil was denied but went anyway, then voluntarily spoke to the bureau in New York after he got back. According to the federal agent, Virgil Griffith said the following:

> Griffith and other attendees discussed how blockchain and cryptocurrency technology could be used by the DPRK [Democratic People's Republic

of Korea, the state's official name] to launder money and evade sanctions, and how the DPRK could use these technologies to achieve independence from the global banking system. . . .

After the DPRK Cryptocurrency Conference, Griffith began formulating plans to facilitate the exchange of Cryptocurrency-1 between the DPRK and South Korea. Griffith acknowledged that assisting with such an exchange would violate sanctions.

As well, "Griffith showed FBI agents photographs of himself in the DPRK and provided to FBI propaganda from the DPRK, including newspapers and other literature," the bureau said. It boggles the mind as to why Virgil did all of that. Every police and legal television show and movie tells you to never voluntarily speak to the authorities. The "first felon" Charlie Shrem, for example, had kept his mouth shut. But Virgil felt differently. Maybe he considered it his patriotic duty to give a debrief to his government. He was, after all, a special breed among a special breed.

In North Korea, it had taken me only a few conversations to believe Virgil definitely had a higher IQ than me. And I witnessed a myriad of his detailed analyses to the locals of seemingly mundane outside-world phenomenon, everything from legalized prostitution to North American slang, such as saying one was doing something appearance-wise "for the ladies." The subtleties of human and societal interaction, the causes and effects and phenomenon of life many process only subconsciously — Virgil could offer intricate and easy-to-understand explanations on the fly. And, of course, he had a doctorate. But

Virgil also suffered from what I'd seen in many smart people. He pondered openly about all sorts of ideas and events and asked questions of the North Koreans that were sensitive to bordering on offensive. Virgil had a hungry curiosity and an unflinching transparency, and a belief that others were like that as well. That turned out to be a hit among the North Koreans, to be sure, and for the longest time after the trip, I thought I should try to be more like Virgil. But put such broad-minded openness in a room with a federal agent, and you often get trouble. It was easy to get over the initial shock of Virgil's arrest. If any one of the eight that had gone to that North Korean blockchain conference were to be arrested, it was going to be him.

One meeting wasn't enough for Virgil. Almost half a year after he talked to the FBI, he talked to agents again in San Francisco, according to the official complaint. A magazine editor for whom Virgil wrote — real name Eric Corley, but who goes by the pseudonym Emmanuel Goldstein, after the enemy of the authoritarian state in *1984* — said on Twitter that Virgil "insisted on going to the @FBI and telling the truth w/o a lawyer. I kept warning him it was a trap." Virgil took little heed, thinking everything was okay.

But there is, I like to think, a part within all of us that likes to embellish travel stories. There is a Marco Polo inside everyone. I myself had been particularly enthusiastic about telling people of my time in that walled garden, even though I'd left the conference without any new cryptocurrency knowledge. I don't know what Virgil thought he told the FBI, but the bureau's takeaway from the meeting was almost painful to read:

> He stated, in sum and substance, that the DPRK government approved the topics within his presentation in advance and that, in his estimation, attendees

left the DPRK Cryptocurrency Conference with a better understanding than when they arrived.

Griffith acknowledged that his presentation at the DPRK Cryptocurrency Conference amounted to a "non-zero tech transfer," that is, a transfer of technical knowledge from Griffith to other attendees.

The same day, Virgil Griffith consented in writing to let the FBI search his phone, and the messages the bureau said it found were not pretty. "Griffith discussed his presentation with another individual," the FBI said. That person was later revealed through court documents to be Virgil's mother. What interest did North Koreans have in cryptocurrency? she asked. "Griffith replied, in sum and substance, 'probably avoiding sanctions . . . who knows.'" Then Virgil told someone else he wanted to send cryptocurrency to North Korea, the FBI said. "In response, Individual-2 asked, in sum and substance, 'Isn't that violating sanctions?' Griffith replied, 'it is.'"

Perhaps Virgil was joking, but the FBI did not see it that way. Virgil eventually hired Brian Klein, the same lawyer who had defended Charlie Shrem in a civil suit, in which the man had been accused of owing $32 million in Bitcoin to the Winklevoss twins who had backed his BitInstant brokerage, a matter later privately settled. It appeared Virgil had smartened up. That arrest in Los Angeles had been a rude reminder of the dangers in that new world he chose, of the "ironic" nature of his unsuspecting interactions with police, as described by his magazine-editor friend Corley. Klein told the court that while Virgil did not deny he went to North Korea, the sanctions-violation charges against him were baseless. In a public statement, Klein said: "We dispute the untested allegations in the criminal complaint. Virgil looks forward to his day in court, when the full story can come out." I had a chat with Klein's colleagues, who provided no additional comment. I also reached out to the North Koreans, but did not hear back.

Virgil's potential twenty years in jail fell somewhere between Charlie Shrem's sentence of two and life imprisonment for Ross Ulbricht, the man behind the Silk Road illicit marketplace. There was a loose connection between the latter two. Shrem's case had also touched on Silk Road. All three also shared something else, beyond the fact that they had involved the same U.S. Attorney's Office for the Southern District of New York: many quarters of the cryptocurrency world felt for them. The three were seen as different from those arrested for running scams, hacking, or stealing electricity to mine cryptocurrency, those accused of taking what was not theirs or causing direct harm to people. To many, Shrem's only crime had been a sloppy running of his Bitcoin brokerage business, a disregard for the identities of his customers and sources of their funds. One had been a prominent Silk Road broker. Ulbricht had believed people should have the freedom to buy whatever drugs they wanted, as long as they were not hurting others. As for Virgil — in the view of those who had been at the conference, at least — he had neither benefited North Korea nor derived any benefit himself. Virgil was only "a typical hacker who loves technology and adventure," his friend Corley told the *New York Times*.

Their wildly differing cases notwithstanding, those three each reflected in some way an important aspect of the cryptocurrency identity. Even if Shrem's disregard for anti–money-laundering rules had been intentional, as the justice department had said, many in the early Bitcoin community had responded, "So

what?" That renegade impulse had been widely indifferent to —
or even supportive of — Ulbricht's jacked-up view of freedom.
Even as new entrants over the years held more tempered views,
even with the great diversity within cryptocurrency, the essence
of Ulbricht's idea was universal. Varying levels of nonconfor-
mity and idealism beat in every crypto heart. This is, after all,
frontierland, a new world built and populated by those who had
deliberately sought to do so, and it has given them community,
wealth, and influence. But unshackled from previous worlds,
disregarding norms, those who walk this valley so surefootedly
sometimes forget what circles overhead.

It was the day after Thanksgiving when we, the rest of the eight
that were in Pyongyang, found out the news from the justice
department's press release. That Black Friday, the news of Virgil's
arrest sent a gloom through our Telegram chat group. To be sure,
we had no reason to be particularly worried that, you know, today
Virgil, tomorrow us. The law Virgil had been accused of breaking
applied only to Americans, and none of us was one. Even if we
were Americans, none of us had any blockchain technical expertise to be accused of imparting to the North Koreans anyway.
To my knowledge, none of us had had interaction with the FBI
at the time, and all of us conference goers had gone to North
Korea not as presenters but simply as passive attendees. It was
extremely unlikely the U.S. government was interested in anyone
else, and I did enter the country later without even the slightest
issue. But while I will not go into why, some in the group might
have felt they had more cause for concern than others. Suddenly,
this Wild West just no longer seemed so fun, filled with candy
mountains and lemonade springs. When I told the former
Oleum contractor Elias Ahonen about the events, he responded:

"Damn. Shit's suddenly serious." One of the conference goers ended up a prosecution witness. With Virgil's arrest, I felt as if something had ended — a loss of innocence, the twilight of an age, the closing of a chapter of my life.

And, as the saying goes, another opened.

When a friend from school learned of my stories, she said, "It's hard to believe you went through all that, part of which was during the time we were at university together." We had not been particularly close. All the saga, all of my highs and lows, the people I met, and the upheaval in the industry — to my friend, it had been invisible, packed beneath the polite chitchat and few words we'd exchanged in our undergraduate feature-writing course, packed into me, a minor character in the story of her life.

The entire business of the North Korea trip wasn't supposed to be in this book. Despite my enthusiasm in telling those around me about it, I knew I had gained no insight into any cryptocurrency ambitions of North Korea. But Virgil's arrest made me view everything about the trip in new light — and not only that. That event made me think a lot, and it hardened my long-held desire to write about my journey as a whole and the other stories of this domain of cryptocurrency. I'd come to see that, despite how much of it was hidden from everyday view, the events of this world had increasingly wide implications for those outside it.

The following is extracted from the actual document. It has been selectively excerpted for length, but is otherwise unedited. All allegations were unproven at the time the document was produced.

SOUTHERN DISTRICT OF NEW YORK, ss.:

BRANDON M. CAVANAUGH, being duly sworn, deposes and says that he is a Special Agent with the Federal Bureau of Investigation (the "FBI"), and charges as follows:

Griffith's May 22, 2019 Admissions

On or about May 22, 2019, I participated in a consensual interview of VIRGIL GRIFFITH, the defendant, in Manhattan, New York (the "May 22 Interview").

GRIFFITH knew that it was illegal to travel to the DPRK and so sought permission from the U.S. Department of State to travel to the DPRK. Although GRIFFITH's request was denied by the State Department, GRIFFITH attended the DPRK Cryptocurrency Conference nonetheless.

GRIFFITH showed FBI agents photographs of himself in the DPRK and provided to FBI propaganda from the DPRK, including newspapers and other literature.

Griffith's Electronic Communications

Based on my participation in this investigation, I know that on or about November 12, 2019, VIRGIL GRIFFITH, the defendant, consented in writing to a search of his cellphone.

On or about November 26, 2018, GRIFFITH discussed his presentation with another individual ("Individual-1") through electronic phone messages. Individual-1 asked, in sum and substance, what interest North Koreans had in cryptocurrency. GRIFFITH replied, in sum and substance, "probably avoiding sanctions . . . who knows."

Griffith's November 12, 2019 Admissions

I know from my participation in this investigation that on or about November 12, 2019, myself and another FBI agent conducted a consensual interview of GRIFFITH in San Francisco, California.

GRIFFITH acknowledged that his presentation at the DPRK Cryptocurrency Conference amounted to a "non-zero tech transfer," that is, a transfer of technical knowledge from GRIFFITH to other attendees.

GRIFFITH expressed a desire to obtain citizenship in another jurisdiction.

CHAPTER 37

In Calgary, I looked deeper and deeper into the local crypto-currency space as I wrote this book, piecing together all the events that had played out earlier, the plots in which I had been only a passerby. Of particular interest was Jan Cerato. A man who had been through his fair share, who'd found a new life in a new world, found fortune, yet found also the messier elements and attracted the attention of the law — I felt his was a story bigger than himself, that it reflected parts of crypto-blockchain and some of the people who comprise it, and that there was a public interest in knowing both the potential and pitfalls of that domain. Other stories, of course, reflect other facets of crypto-blockchain, and learning such tales is what truly helps to understand it all. To the outsider, especially, what is crucial is not any technical, nuts-and-bolts discourse — who really can explain electricity or the internet or even cares about such explanations? — but the stories of the people and their lives in and around this new world.

I had planned to reach out to Jan for comment, to give him a heads-up that he would be in my book, and to hear his side of the story if he wanted to say it. But, before I could do so, Jan reached out to me. He had found out I was looking into him. That was not in itself unexpected. It had happened for Louise Panneton at the Alberta Securities Commission as well. When you talk to people around a man, someone will tell him. Jan sent me a strange text message whose premise was loaded and dubious: "Hey Etard we have copies of your text messages harassing my friends, my law firm would like your address so we they [sic] can send you some information asap. Text the info here so we can make sure your [sic] aware of the consequences. Thank you."

I eventually reached out to the lawyer Jan had been known to use, the same Cameron Bally who had once sued him, and the attorney did not immediately get back to me. But I did not respond to Jan's text that called me "Etard." I'd wanted to have a face-to-face conversation. It's something journalists always desire, to pose questions in a dynamic back-and-forth with our subject. The hostility Jan displayed in his message seemed to stand in the way of that. But I like to think of myself as personable, with a certain disarming manner that may not come across as readily in a text message. Maybe in person, Jan would be less hostile to me, I thought, as I signed up for one of his events on Meetup.com one Thursday in late 2019. One rule of journalism is to be transparent. And personally, being viewed as duplicitous is what I hate most. I telegraph my intentions as much as I can. As much as I can, I do not want people to feel accosted.

That was a bad idea. Jan saw that I had signed up for his meetup and immediately kicked me out and banned me from ever registering for his Meetup.com group again (although I later did join again). Then Jan sent a bizarre message to the group, telling its more than 1,000 members that "authorities are tracking the phones of people posing as" a group of people that included me — "be extremely careful if they have contacted you, sent you messages or phone calls." He continued, without providing evidence or rationale, "Apparently they are being investigated and we need all the data sent to our office."

Oh, well. So much for being honest. It appeared I would not be expecting any welcome at the casino. But judging from Jan's reaction to everything, I felt my chances of speaking to him in person were only going to go down from there. I could call, email, or text whenever I fancied, but if I wanted to have a face-to-face conversation — if it did not happen that day, it would probably never happen. Might as well get it over with. I had nothing to lose, and talking to him, getting his side of the story, was something that had to be done anyway, regardless of how uncomfortable it might be. I walked into the casino's Japanese restaurant that evening with a purpose pounding within me firm yet fast. I emailed a friend that I was there doing that, and she responded: "Eeeeek!!! Do you need back-up?!?!"

Jan was not there.

In the Kabuki lounge of the restaurant, there were only two attendees. While a handful more would arrive later, all in all, the turnout was a far cry from the meetup's glory days. Also present was someone who helped Jan with his presentations, carrying a look both simian and reptile. I recognized no one. Jan was late. I left the lounge and sat waiting by one of the restaurant's empty teppanyaki grills.

Outside, darkness gathered in the clear air, and the casino crimson was stark against the sky. It was the sort of evening in which everything was stark. Sound traveled well, and so did the coming winter.

Jan came in carrying assorted presentation materials, wearing a black T-shirt that read "will work for Bitcoin" in white sans serif font, with a white border around the words, and he had on a black Bitcoin hat and camouflage pants.

"Jan." I started to walk toward him.

"Yes?" There was a sort of expressiveness in Jan's face. I could see him searching the recesses of his memory, hunting for the event from his past that would identify me. As if happening in slow motion, I could see the smile fade and contort into displeasure as he recognized me.

"We need to talk," I said. Jan was a little taller than me, so I tried to stand straighter.

"Not a chance."

The conversation fell apart from there. Jan went from saying he had no time to talk to believing he had the ability to eject me from the restaurant. "Do you want me to talk to security?"

"You are entitled to do whatever you feel is right, but I'm not your enemy here."

At that point Jan walked away, heading into his meetup, during which he would say that Cloud Token, the questionable investment he had been promoting, would have "a velocity now moving into 2020" and would "pick up so much pace."

Somehow, before that interaction with Jan, I thought I would have been charm itself, rakishly persuasive, riding with dash, acting with flair, smooth as axel grease. But clearly I was wrong. In Jan's view, perhaps, I was as charming as a trout. I did not follow him.

Days later, I had a phone call with Jan, in which he said he had to be paid to be written about. "I'm a registered corporation," he said. "I don't even know if you know what that means." He eventually hung up on me. I subsequently approached Jan twice through mutual contacts, each time via a different one, both of whom were on good terms with him, one of whom was the former Oleum contractor Elias Ahonen. I also sent Jan four emails — one of which laid out everything in more than 5,000 words — repeatedly telling him I wanted to hear his side of the story. I phoned Jan again, and he rejected the call. We then had a text exchange. Between insults — calling me a "slut" with "no food" — Jan at first said there was "no investigation" into him before saying that the Alberta Securities Commission had, in his view, cleared him. Jan also compared the two of us using the benchmark of Meetup.com, saying he had "finished 100 meetups" and in his view had been "doing amazing things," whereas I had derived no material benefit from the informal gatherings of my buddies and me at the pub: "Where are your customers and fans?? You have none, your [sic] a loser." I did not engage with Jan on any of his insults, sticking only to the facts and reiterating I would welcome his comment on anything and everything in this book and in whatever medium he preferred. Jan asked for an apology, without elaborating on why he felt one was necessary, and did not respond when I said I would not give one.

One of the discoveries I'd made in my investigations, though, was that the people interested in Jan's activities numbered far more than I'd thought.

CHAPTER 38

Night spread from the northeast like a cast net, over the stars, bright and brittle in the chilly air. Toward the end of 2019, as the days grew shorter, the pressure on Jan increased, and his world shrank. His original business associates had long left. He and his girlfriend, the musician Angie Coombes, would break up. Jan had, as well, been explicitly excluded from a new industry consortium in Calgary. Then Jan made an appearance on a well-known user-submitted badmouthing website in a post related to his cryptocurrency dealings. It was anonymous and unproven but clearly involved above-average effort, complete with graphic design, indicating whoever posted it had a white-hot vendetta.

Meanwhile, the law had come into town again: the federal police, officially called the Royal Canadian Mounted Police, the successor force of the 50 men in red coats that Captain Éphrem-A. Brisebois brought over some 150 years earlier. These new Mounties have units called Integrated Market Enforcement Teams to combat financial crime. In my city, they holed themselves up in an aluminum- and green-roofed little building near the airport. It was nondescript, single-story, with mirrored windows and without any police logos outside, and if you leaned against its beige-brown bricks, sooner or later someone would ask you to state your business. At an event in the city, Inspector Charlene O'Neill, who handled local financial crimes, said the feds were hiring an analyst and a technical specialist in the area to deal with cryptocurrency. While there was still no official news about the Alberta Securities Commission investigation into Jan, sources directly briefed on the matter told me the regulator had referred the case to the federal police, and the cops were investigating.

To be sure, federal criminal charges need to meet a much higher bar than the commission's administrative enforcement measures. My sources said the police were not yet alleging any wrongdoing by anyone, and it is anyone's guess if they get there. In accordance with protocol, the feds declined to comment on their investigation, much like the commission that referred the case to them. Jan told me Cameron Bally, his lawyer, could speak to his innocence. But that thought clearly did not make it to the attorney, who said he was "unable to discuss these matters" without his client's consent. In text messages to me, though, Jan was emphatic and detailed in his belief of innocence, saying "all intersested [sic] parties found out that im not doing anything wrong or illegal." He added that it was "the ones who were jealous and kicked out of my club" that had "spread the lies and hate." He did not specify if it was the whaleclub or a figurative club. Jan said it was only "cowards" that had contacted federal police and the Alberta Securities Commission, and that both authorities had come to "know" that their time had been wasted on the matter.

But the products associated with Jan garnered increasing attention. Daniel Pacheco, the founder of iPro Network — whose earlier event had listed Jan as an organizer — ended up sued by the U.S. Securities and Exchange Commission, although he denied the allegations. "IPro raised more than $26 million," the commission said, spelling the name with a capital *I*. "However, IPro was a fraudulent pyramid scheme. IPro's inevitable collapse was hastened by Pacheco's fraudulent use of investor funds, which included, among other things, the all-cash purchase of a $2.5 million home and a Rolls Royce." Cloud Token also collapsed, and it incurred the wrath of authorities all across the world, from Mauritius to Taiwan. None of those cases involved Jan personally, but Facebook banned him from posting about Cloud for a while. Then the B.C. Securities Commission, on the West Coast, warned against the product, and while it did not name anyone — and there is no evidence Jan was on its radar — the regulator said, "One of the people promoting Cloud Wallet in online forums lives in Canada." Then the Alberta Securities Commission issued a notice of hearing against Jan, formally accusing him of illegally distributing securities through the "Whale Club," which the regulator spelled with two words. Then the commission investigator Dale Fisher, who had probed the whaleclub together with Louise Panneton, turned his attention to Cloud. Jan posted on his blog that "Feds" had "influenced the banksters to close my accounts" and that his credit score had been "ruined."

In another blog post, while Jan did not address Cloud, just as how he did not address it when I had raised the matter with him, he reiterated his stances on the other issues. Jan said he had nothing to do with iPro Network, and that he had not been in charge of the whaleclub, had been roped in unaware of the full picture, and had played only a minor role. Jan disparaged former business associates, for whom he used only first names, and an unnamed "low-level" commission investigator that, in the version of the post sent over Telegram, he fingered more specifically as "Dale the D-bag." Jan also named an "Ethan" that he called an "odd guy" and "not very intelligent." In Jan's view, he was a "well respected [sic] businessman . . . antagonized by the lack of fact checking" on the part of the commission, unfairly targeted in a world in which many felt "envy/jealousy" toward him. He wrote, "Bad style was everywhere and everyone wanted to be me, the guy who had all the people chasing him for his teachings and strategies" — and I have no doubt that Jan genuinely and strongly believed that. We are all, after all, the main characters of our own epics.

I attended Jan's whaleclub hearing before the Alberta Securities Commission hoping to hear from him, but he was not required to be there, and he wasn't. Jan did have a lawyer present, but not one that was previously known to me. Over two weeks, I heard witness after witness tell the commission the same as they had told me: they were no experts in cryptocurrency, wanted to make some profit in that new world, but lost money through the whaleclub. Loss is, of course, to be expected of any financial venture, and that in itself does not signal anything improper on the part of any investment club. And those claims of loss would likely never be tested, for the charge against Jan was based only on the narrow technicality that he allegedly did not have the proper paperwork for offering the relevant investments. Jan's lawyer said at the hearing the commission's accusation was without merit, and he raised what he said were procedural issues. Nothing at all has been proven as I write this. But what is certain is that whether witnesses say they lost money or not, the commission does not care.

In late 2020, amid a global pandemic, an again-booming Bitcoin surpassed its earlier peak of $20,000, and in the ensuing year it surged even more, repeatedly attaining new all-time highs, sparked by both institutional and retail interest. The Coinbase exchange, which in 2017 became the first cryptocurrency company to be worth $1 billion, was valued at $100 billion by the time it planned for a public offering in 2021. Ethereum became hot again for yet another use case: the non-fungible token (NFT), essentially a way to ensure virtual objects cannot be simply copied. One resulting digital artwork ended up selling for nearly $70 million at the auction house Christie's. To purists, of course, all of that is immaterial — companies rise and fall; Bitcoin may well plunge back down, for such turbulence is to be expected; and Ethereum fads come and go — what is important is the growing recognition that this represents a technology that may change the world.

When I think about everything I've seen and gone through in the cryptocurrency world, though, I always think back to that summer when I cycled past the river Bow outside my apartment and noticed for the first time the driftwood on its stony shores, riding in on the crests of the booming waters, then left beached when the waves waned. At the time, I had just learned a disturbing fact. The *Globe and Mail* newspaper had just reported on a tributary waterway with the headline saying "officials seek source of river pollution after three years of elevated bacteria levels." The article filled in a key detail that did not make it into the headline. What kind of bacteria was it? It was the fecal kind. For three years, the city had warned the public, but why or how there was so much shit in the water was a mystery it had never solved. All the same, people paddled the river. Their dogs dived and dipped in the discharge. The rapids flowed forth, ceaseless and ceaselessly moving. And there seemed to be a little bit more driftwood each year. Gray, haggard, and weathered, tossed by the wind and dulled and eroded by rain, it piled on the riverbank.

I do see the beauty in this realm of cryptocurrency and believe there will be an order to its days, a purpose. But there is also an ugliness, a disarray that is the inevitable price of change, strangely analogous to that of under-policed American small towns, about which the article "Outlaw Country" in *Atavist Magazine* says, "The social contract is not a buffet — if you opt out because you want absolute freedom, you have to accept that no one will come to save your ass when trouble starts." A new world is rising, and nothing, no system, no improvement in living, ever came without trial, pain, and struggle. In telling these stories, I hope new entrants will have a clearer path, that through my journey, I've brought back and have done something of value, and that I have made this world better.

One Christmas Eve, Jan proclaimed his exit from this new industry for the second time, sending a message to his Meetup.com group saying he was "retiring completely from Crypto Currency 100%." He wrote about himself in the third person: "Jan felt it was important to End all ties to people, places & things that were not producing the proper Positive results he was looking for especially from various people in the community." In the days to come, Jan Gregory Cerato followed up by removing his last name from his social media profiles, going instead by "Jan Gregory," and stepping down as an organizer from his meetup group.

The group had 1,327 members at the time, the largest of its kind in the city. The day Jan stepped down, every member of the group got an alert. What Meetup.com did when an organizer left was open the position to anyone who wanted to step up, but the catch was you had to have a paid subscription — or else the group would be closed, all of its records purged. For someone writing a book, the group was a piece of history that needed to be preserved. I thought but not a lot. It was early morning when the Meetup.com alert came, but it could also be very late at night, one of those liminal, in-between periods when both coffee and whiskey are appropriate. The wind blew west, fresh from the pines, cold from the mountain snow. While I haven't the faintest clue what precisely I will do with it beyond preserving its records, I now own Jan Cerato's meetup group. ⑧

The following is a text exchange between Ethan Lou and Jan Cerato, presented verbatim. Some names have been redacted as the allegations against those people could not be immediately verified.

Hi Jan, I'm following up on our previous communications and would like to both reiterate and expand on what was said. I remain interested in and committed to hearing what you have to say and aim to portray you fairly in my book. You may have become aware of a investigation into you by the Royal Canadian Mounted Police. I would welcome any comment you may have on that matter, and on any other issues, including your activities in the cryptocurrency space; involvement in investments that have garnered the attention of the regulators; and interactions with the legal system and the authorities.

Go back to sept 2017 when you created your pathetic meetup where you slagged me and disrespected my game, its still online. Meanwhile i just finished 100 meetups!! Where are yours? Where are your customers and fans?? You have none, your a loser look in the mirror! Stop calling me and call the suicide hotline instead!! I'll never give you the time of day until you learn to respect and apologize! Until then Fuck you slut!!

I can understand that I am approaching you with matters that are not what one wants to hear, but this is something that is fully proceeding. These are, as well, matters of the public interest and the bulk of it is already public. If you address these matters, readers will be able to hear your side of the story and will be able to fairly judge the truth of the issues. I believe readers will also see and appreciate your frankness. I can assure you anything you put forth, in whatever medium, will be faithfully represented.

Nothing you are working is True, its all false
rumors and hearsay. Its not worth my time
and you dont deserve to speak to me since
you are a disrespecting loser! When you
change your approach maybe you will get a
chance

You are has-been! Your not relevant, your
not current, nobody knows you or cares
about anything you do! Why would i share
anything with a deadbeat like you? Theres
tons of reports out there doing the Buzz and
the real job. Like i said your a waste of time.
Losers have no reach and nothing for me to
gain! Bye

I am interested only in the truth and accurate facts and in ensuring that everything I
write is backed up by firm veracity. If you
feel there are any falsehoods or incomplete-
ness in my knowledge — particularly with
respect to the investigations into you by
the Alberta Securities Commission and the
RCMP, which as I am sure you are aware,
are serious matters that will have an impact
on you — I am always open to your input
on what you feel is the correct version of
events. I remain committed to giving you
every opportunity to comment.

You have no job, no accomplishments, no
friends, no fans, no customers, no outlet, no
reach, no klout, no brand, no help, no food,
no money, no Point!! There is no investigation its all rumors! I would know since it
would be involving me right? Theres nothing
to investigate since i havent done anything
wrong right? Cause if i did then maybe the
rumors would hold true, right?

Its not illegal to have meetups, its not illegal
to have a private investment club under
50members, its not illegal to trade bitcoin,

its not illegal to give your friends ideas. So
far like the rcmp, asc, law office and all
intersested parties found out that im not
doing anything wrong or illegal. Call ford
hemington and ask for Cam Bally he will give
you comments in regards to all the asc, rcmp
etc. He will tell you i have done nothing wrong
just like he told all of them the same thing!!

Nothing wrong here! All good and above
the board dealings with all my peeps. The
ones who spread the lies and hate are all
the ones who were jealous and kicked out of
my club!

Do you want to interview them all??

So keep listening to the losers, dont call the
lawyers and get a proper credible statement
of affairs. Just keep believing the bumholes
who hate the man for doing amazing things
for people in the crypto space!! I have 1400
people who love me soooooo much!!

All the cowards called the rcmp and asc to
waste their time and they know that now.
They know everything!

> I did reach out to Bally some months ago,
> although he has not gotten back to me. My
> understanding is that you considered Jeffrey
> Thom of McLeod Law for representation for
> the ASC matter. I imagine eventually it was
> Bally who represented you for that?

The asc matter was actually against [name
redacted] not me, hes the lead on the issue
and the file. I was a asstistant to him, he ran
the dealings and asc was after him not me

Its all in the files at the lawyers

Thats why the fools are totally wrong and
dont even know what the hell they talkin
bout! Im the man so the all the attenion is
on me but im not a concern

Did anyone happen to mention that ive been
retired since 1998 and that crypto was and
is my hobby and side hustle and i dont take
it as serious as most do. I dont care about it
like you think i do. Im using the crypto
movement to my advantage, its my choice
and right to capitalize on the moments.

Im part of a wayyyyy bigger group then you
all realize, this is worldwide movement.
A few idiots in calgary have no idea what
were up to!

When we went to asc office they gave me 25
pages of posts from the web that i supposedly wrote them and posted them and they
were all FAKE they werent me or my accounts. I tossed it back in their pile! [name
redacted] photoshopped them and hes being
pursued currently under subpoena

All the jelaous rats tried to sabotage my
stance but it didnt work! You have to have
real Evidence to make a statement!

What was your interaction with Louise Panneton like?

She quit the day of my interview right after

As in she left the organization or in your view,
after speaking to you, she found no merit in
the case against you she was pursuing?

I didnt let them pin any of their false fake
bullshit on me and she worked for over a

year on that file! She quit moved back to
ontario! My lawyer crushed all if their false
evidence and assumtions!

Yup true story in fact [name redacted] who
was in charge of the so called whale club
applied for her job right after and they
laughed at him

Lol crazy peeps

When i went head to head with them in the
room they were so shook up they couldnt
write with their pens or communicate properly
constantly pausing for breaks, half way
through they knew that i was clean clear and
not involved in anything they thought i was!

> Well, thanks for engaging with me, Jan,
> and giving me your perspective. I will be
> reaching out to Bally again, given that you
> say he represented you in matters including
> the investigations by the ASC and RCMP,.
> There are a lot of other matters on which
> I am writing for which I had been seeking
> your comment, outlined in my email to you
> on Nov. 13 and its attachment, as I'm sure
> you're aware. I will always welcome any
> comment on any of those matters and am
> happy to engage in whatever medium you
> prefer.

Bring your laptop and let's go for coffee

You can start by apologizing to me and then
we can move forward

> I'm happy to go for coffee. Let me know a
> time and a place. I do want to say upfront,
> though, that an apology is not going to
> happen.

AUTHOR'S NOTE

Everything in this book happened. Any speech attributed to a character has actually been said. When I write about people's thoughts, they either were described to me directly or come from words they have said before — publicly available or provided to me in documents or recordings. Some minor characters, whose parts in the book are inconsequential to the narrative, such as a friend from university, are mentioned by partial names or variations so as to respect their privacy. Those are different from the people whose names I have completely withheld for journalistic reasons, because they have provided me sensitive information on a confidential basis, for example — whenever I do so, I have made the reason and context clear in the text.

Extensive primary research — journalistic work — went into this book: accessing public records such as court documents and filing freedom-of-information requests for internal records of law enforcement and regulators, for example. At one point, I was looking at 25 court cases that I tracked with a spreadsheet. The investigator Louise Panneton's graduate thesis was so old, I had to dig it up in microform from a library 2,000 miles away. This book also involved interviews with more than 100 people. That is a rough estimate because, honestly, I have lost count. Some of those people were confidential sources. For some of the book's subjects, I was also granted materials that were not ordinarily publicly available, such as instant-messaging chat logs, by people who had access. I abided by ethical and legal standards.

Secondary sources I used are mostly publicly available ones, such as media and academic and historical files, laying out established and uncontroversial facts. They come in two varieties. The first comprise those that enable me to spin a good yarn: geographical and meteorological records that tell me which way the wind was blowing on a particular day, or what sort of trees grow on what riverbank or mountain; historical facts such as how many buffalo robes a gallon of whiskey fetched, what sort of past this or that city has, or how much money changed hands in horse-racing bets on this particular day in the nineteenth century; and cultural products such as books, movies, and televisions shows that I invoke or from which I quote to make certain points — that is, sources that serve only as color, to brighten an otherwise dull tale.

The other type of secondary sources provide general information related to the events of the book, such as the price journey of Bitcoin and the major events associated with the industry, or biographical information on notable people in the space; the backgrounds of the characters and the events with which they were involved prior to the timeline of the book, such as the police raid and subsequent restaurant killings depicted in the prologue; and just general facts and statistics about the world, such as what proportion of Thai millennials are in debt, or how many times North Korea has been subject to economic sanctions.

I have not done any citations or endnotes, which is in line with the convention of works of journalism. The thrust of the book derives largely from reportage. For most information, I have clearly stated the sources within the book, such as an interview, legal proceedings, a text message sent to me, or chat log shown to me. I have gone to extensive lengths to show my work within the writing. I also firmly believe that nobody ever reads this section of a book.

I have, however, included a selected bibliography. It is by no means a comprehensive tabulation, and deliberately so. An entire report from Statistics Canada, for example, from which I reference just one line — I do not feel the inclusion of that here gives the reader much value. In fact, inclusion of every single source like that results in a dump of information that I feel has a neutral, or even negative value. It would be like highlighting every single line in a textbook. I am also admittedly lazy and shortsighted. They say to do the citations as you write. I never listen, to my shame. I have therefore taken great care not to overload the reader with the bibliography. I have selected some sources that I believe provide for useful further reading and add context and background to some of the events depicted in this book. The criterion for inclusion is mainly how valuable the sources would be as stand-alone works — that is, if readers will find them interesting even if they have not flipped through this book.

SELECTED BIBLIOGRAPHY

PROLOGUE

Gilchrist, John. "Determined Owners Take Back Their Restaurant." *Calgary Herald*, March 15, 2009.

Kauffman, Bill. "Killer of Bystander in Gangland Bolsa Slayings Pleads for Forgiveness." *Calgary Herald*, April 13, 2016.

Massinon, Stephane. "Bombs Found in Luxury Home; Five Face Charges in Gang Bust." *Calgary Herald*, December 24, 2008.

Martin, Kevin. "Gang Violence Sexually Aroused Accused Massacre Participant, Calgary Court Told." *QMI Agency*, March 14, 2012.

ACT I
2013 HIGH: $1,200

CHAPTER 1

DiManno, Rosie. "Mysterious Deaths Make 200 Wellesley E. Toronto's Most Ominous Address: DiManno." *Toronto Star*, January 6, 2014.

Elliott, Francis, and Gary Duncan. "Chancellor on Brink of Second Bailout for Banks." *The Times*, January 3, 2009.

Hunter, Brad. "Dark Web Offered Sex Slave Shopping List."
Toronto Sun, August 8, 2017.

Nakamoto, Satoshi. "Bitcoin: A Peer-to-Peer Electronic Cash
System." October 31, 2008.

Weimann, Gabriel. "Terrorist Migration to the Dark Web."
Perspectives on Terrorism, Vol. 10, No. 3 (2016): 40-44.

CHAPTER 2

Hobbs, Michael. "Why Millennials Are Facing the Scariest
Financial Future of any Generation since the Great
Depression." *HuffPost*. Accessed August 7, 2019.

McMillan, Robert. "The Inside Story of Mt. Gox, Bitcoin's
$460 Million Disaster." *Wired*, March 3, 2014.

Pachner, Joanna. "Livin' Large with Canada's Crypto King."
Globe and Mail, November 27, 2018.

Popper, Nathaniel. *Digital Gold: Bitcoin and the Inside Story
of the Misfits and Millionaires Trying to Reinvent Money.*
HarperCollins: New York, 2015.

Sarner, Jamie. "The Seven Ugliest Buildings in Toronto." *Jamie
Sarner*, August 26, 2011.

CHAPTER 3

Frankenfield, Jake. "HODL." *Investopedia*. Dotdash. Accessed
June 25, 2019.

Lou, Ethan. "Is It Loonie to Collect Your Salary in Bitcoin?"
Canadian Press, September 2, 2014.

Merchant, Brian. "Click Here to Kill." *Harper's Magazine*,
January 2020.

CHAPTER 4

Lou, Ethan. "Bitcoin Guru Leaves Canada's TSX to Focus on
Blockchain Venture." *Reuters*, November 28, 2016.

————. "Canada's TSX Hires Bitcoin Guru, Studies Currency's Technology." *Reuters*, March 4, 2016.

Rizzo, Pete. "$100k Peter Thiel Fellowship Awarded to Ethereum's Vitalik Buterin." *CoinDesk*, June 5, 2014.

ACT II
2017 HIGH: $20,000

CHAPTER 5

Graveland, Bill. "Police Say Increasing Domestic Abuse in Calgary Tied to Economic Downturn." *Canadian Press*, November 1, 2016.

Krotoski, Aleks. "Where Does Amazon's Alexa Get Her News From?" *Financial Times*, January 10, 2020.

Stenson, Fred. *The Story of Calgary*. Saskatoon, Saskatchewan: Fifth House, 1994.

Williams, Nia. "Oil Price Plunge Pulling Calgary's Housing Market Down with It." *Reuters*, March 5, 2015.

CHAPTER 6

BehindMLM. "Is iPro Network a proxy for OneCoin's US Ponzi scammers?" March 10, 2017.

Castillo, Michelle. "This High School Dropout Who Invested in Bitcoin at $12 Is Now a Millionaire at 18." *CNBC*, June 20, 2019.

Morris, David Z. "The Rise of Cryptocurrency Ponzi Schemes." *The Atlantic*, May 31, 2017.

PM_Poutine. "Here Is a List of Crypto Ponzi Schemes and People Who Are/Were Promoting Them on YouTube." *Reddit*, January 17, 2018.

Rosario, Nelson. "OneCoin Operations Harm Allegedly 'Exceeds $4 Billion.'" *The Block*, May 12, 2019.

CHAPTER 8

Foran, Max. *Calgary: Canada's Frontier Metropolis, An Illustrated History.* Burlington, Ontario: Windsor Publications, 1982.

Huang, Roger. "How Bitcoin and WikiLeaks Saved Each Other." *Forbes*, April 26, 2019.

Notable Life. "Jan G. Cerato: Today's Notable Young Entrepreneur." February 24, 2015.

ACT III
2018 HIGH: $17,700

CHAPTER 12

Deahl, Dani, and Shannon Liao. "Why Dennis Rodman Promoted Potcoin at a North Korea Summit." *The Verge*, June 12, 2019.

Hajdarbegovic, Nermin. "Kanye West Sues Coinye Altcoin into Oblivion." *CoinDesk*, July 29, 2014.

Higgins, Stan. "SEC: Celebrity ICO Endorsements Could Be Illegal." *CoinDesk*, November 1, 2017.

CHAPTER 13

Griffith, Erin. "Is Your Startup Stalled? Pivot to Blockchain." *Wired*, January 3, 2018.

Hackett, Robert. "Coinbase Becomes First Bitcoin 'Unicorn.'" *Fortune*, August 10, 2017.

Maclean, Jason. "HIVE Blockchain Has an 88 Per Cent Upside, GMP says." *Cantech Letter*, January 29, 2018.

Shapira, Arie, and Kailey Leinz. "Long Island Iced Tea Soars After Changing Its Name to Long Blockchain." *Bloomberg*, December 21, 2017.

Shufelt, Tim. "Marijuana Stocks, Blockchain Transform Canada's Investing Landscape." *Globe and Mail*, January 12, 2018.

CHAPTER 14

Cerato, Jan. "Sergio Cerato RIP." *The Life and Times of JantheMan*, June 20, 2012.

Lecacheur, Julien. "Medical Marijuana Still Divides Doctors, but Calgary Patients Swear by the Drug." *CBC*, November 27, 2016.

Macdonald, Ross. "Jan Cerato / Bitcoin Influencer." *Crypto Culture Magazine*, October 2018.

Zetter, Kim. "How the Feds Took Down the Silk Road Drug Wonderland." *Wired*, November 18, 2013.

CHAPTER 16

Associated Press. "Bitcoins Worth $100K Stolen over Public Wireless Network." November 27, 2017.

Cointelegraph. "Report on Crypto Exchange Hacks." Accessed June 20, 2020.

Duhaime, Christine. "Murder and Violent Robberies of Digital Currency Executives up over 100% in 2018 as Bitcoin Exchange Owner Murdered, and another ICO Founder Assaulted and Robbed at Gun Point." *Duhaime's Anti–Money Laundering and Financial Crime News*, July 8, 2018.

Sedgwick, Kai. "How to Survive a Blockchain Conference without Getting Hacked." *Bitcoin.com*, May 10, 2018.

Zuckerman, Molly Jane. "Russian Crypto Developer Beaten, Robbed of 300 BTC on Moscow Streets." *Cointelegraph*, February 27, 2018.

CHAPTER 17

Cheng, Evelyn, and Kate Rooney. "Bitcoin Conferences Flood New York, Bringing Millions in Ticket Sales." *CNBC*, May 13, 2018.

Gin, Zarc. "Why Blockchain Industry Has a Conference Fever." *Daily Fintech*, August 25, 2018.

INTERMISSION
NORTH KOREA

CHAPTER 18

Copeland, Tim. "North Korea Is Mining Way More Monero than Last Year." *Decrypt*, February 11, 2020.

Economist. "America's Aggressive Use of Sanctions Endangers the Dollar's Reign." January 18, 2020.

Kang, Tae-jun. "A Closer Look at North Korea's Virtual Currency Ambitions." *The Diplomat*, April 19, 2019.

————. "How Far Has North Korea Come With Cryptocurrency?" *The Diplomat*, September 7, 2018.

Mallonee, Laura. "All Aboard Air Koryo, North Korea's Fleet of Ancient Soviet Planes." *Wired*, June 19, 2017.

Yoshida, Kaori. "North Korea Stole Cryptocurrency via Hacking: UN Panel." *Nikkei*, March 8, 2019.

CHAPTER 19

Choe, Sang-Hun. "Time Is Running Out for Trump's North Korean Diplomacy, Analysts Say." *New York Times*, November 28, 2019.

Fifield, Anna. "North Korea Issued $2 Million Bill for Comatose Otto Warmbier's Care." *Washington Post*, April 24, 2019.

Keneally, Meghan. "From 'Fire and Fury' to 'Rocket Man,' the Various Barbs Traded between Trump and Kim Jong-un." *ABC News*, June 12, 2018.

Kramer, Andrew E., and Choe Sang-Hun. "After Meeting Kim Jong-un, Putin Supports North Korea on Nuclear Disarmament." *New York Times*, April 25, 2019.

Moxley, Mitch. "Rent a White Guy." *The Atlantic*, July/August 2010.

Yan, Alice. "White People Wanted: A Peek into China's Booming 'Rent a Foreigner' Industry." *South China Morning Post*, June 10, 2017.

ACT IV
2018 LOW: $3,200

CHAPTER 20

Castor, Amy. "Interview with Roger Ver: His Plans to Start a New Libertarian Country." *Bitcoin Magazine*, September 25, 2017.

Kharpal, Arjun. "WikiLeaks Founder Assange Claims He Made 50,000% Return on Bitcoin Thanks to the US Government." *CNBC*, October 16, 2017.

King, Georgia Frances. "The Venn Diagram between Libertarians and Crypto Bros is so Close It's Basically a Circle." *Quartz*, May 23, 2018.

Nakamoto, Satoshi. "Bitcoin P2P e-cash paper." Cryptography Mailing List, November 14, 2008.

Okotoks Today. "Candidate tackling unorthodox issues." April 20, 2011.

CHAPTER 21

O'Hagan, Andrew. *The Secret Life: Three True Stories*. London: Faber and Faber, 2017.

BTC Sessions. "Tales from The Bitcoin Rodeo." YouTube video, July 24, 2018.

CHAPTER 22

Gomez, Miguel. "Almost 1 in 5 Investors Are Going into Debt to Buy Bitcoin." *Cryptovest*, January 13, 2018.

———. "Chinese Firms Selling Crypto Mining Equipment by Weight." *Cryptovest*, November 23, 2018.

Park, Elly. "Bitcoin Rises Ten Percent after Brutal Selloff." *Reuters* video, December 26, 2017.

Premack, Rachel. "South Korean Millennials Are Reeling from the Bitcoin Bust." *The Verge*, April 3, 2018.

CHAPTER 23

Donaldson, Jesse. "The Lengths People Will Go to Avoid Getting 'Served.'" *Vice*, September 27, 2017.

Sameday Process. "The Life of a Process Server." November 8, 2019.

ACT V
2019 LOW: $3,400

CHAPTER 24

Alberta Securities Commission. "Employee Expense Claim." November 8, 2018.

Panneton, Louise. "L'obligation d'information du médecin et son impact sur la vie de couple." Master's thesis, Université de Montréal, 1996.

CHAPTER 26

Alberta Securities Commission. Enforcement Manual. August 13, 2012.

Busch, Lionel, and Mike Mumby. "Enhancing Enforcement — Effective Interviewing." Alberta Securities Commission, slideshow, September 12, 2019.

Calgary Herald. "Making the Case for More Legal Aid Funding." October 27, 2014.

CHAPTER 27

Baldwin, Clare. "Bitcoin Worth $72 Million Stolen from Bitfinex Exchange in Hong Kong." *Reuters*, August 3, 2016.

Lee-Young, Joanne. "Bitcoin Investors Face Long Delays Cashing Out, Criticize Two B.C. firms." *Vancouver Sun*, April 15, 2018.

Lou, Ethan. "Another Vancouver-Spawned Bitcoin Firm Accused of Owing Millions." *The Tyee*, July 26, 2019.

Nonomiya, Lily. "$32 Million Swiped from Cryptocurrency Exchange in Latest Hack." *Bloomberg*, July 12, 2019.

Posadzki, Alexandra. "Judge Rules with CIBC, Grants Possession of Disputed Quadriga Funds to Ontario Superior Court." *Globe and Mail*, November 13, 2018.

Popper, Nathaniel. "Owners of BitMEX, a Leading Bitcoin Exchange, Face Criminal Charges." *New York Times*, October 1, 2020.

CHAPTER 28

Alexander, Doug. "Software Engineer Loses Life Savings in Quadriga Imbroglio." *Bloomberg*, February 9, 2019.

Castaldo, Joe, and Alexandra Posadzki. "Before Quadriga: How Shady Ventures in Gerald Cotten's Youth Led to the Creation of His Ill-Fated Cryptocurrency Exchange." November 22, 2019.

———. "Lawyers for Quadriga Customers Ask RCMP to Exhume Founder Gerald Cotten's Body." *Globe and Mail*, December 13, 2019.

Castaldo, Joe, Alexandra Posadzki, Jessica Leeder, and Lindsay Jones. "Crypto Chaos: From Vancouver to Halifax, Tracing

the Mystery of Quadriga's Missing Millions." *Globe and Mail*, February 8, 2019.

Lou, Ethan. "Are You Buying and Selling Cryptocurrency? Do You See a Future for It? Has the News about QuadrigaCX Changed How You See It?" Interview by Judy Aldous. *CBC*, February 6, 2019.

Posadzki, Alexandra, and Joe Castaldo. "Quadriga Monitor's Report Offers Strongest Evidence Yet of Fraud, Experts Say." *Globe and Mail*, June 20, 2019.

Rich, Nathaniel. "Ponzi Schemes, Private Yachts, and a Missing $250 Million in Crypto: the Strange Tale of Quadriga." *Vanity Fair*, November 22, 2019.

Vanderklippe, Nathan, Jessica Leeder, and Alexandra Posadzki. "How Did Gerald Cotten Die? A Quadriga Mystery, from India to Canada and Back." *Globe and Mail*, February 15, 2019.

CHAPTER 29

Clark, Bryan. "Celebrity-Endorsed ICOs Are a Dumpster Fire of Epic Proportions." *Hard Fork*, April 6, 2018.

Haig, Samuel. "Report: ICO Fundraising Plummeted 95% Year-Over-Year in 2019." *Cointelegraph*, March 23, 2020.

Kharif, Olga. "Half of ICOs Die Within Four Months After Token Sales Finalized." *Bloomberg*, July 9, 2018.

Robinson, Matt. "Actor Steven Seagal Fined by SEC for Touting Token Offering." *Bloomberg*, February 27, 2020.

Varshney, Neer. "1 in Every 5 ICOs Is Phony, WSJ Study Finds." *Hard Fork*, May 18, 2018.

———. "SEC Sets Up a Fake ICO to Warn Naive Investors against Cryptocurrency Scams." *Hard Fork*, May 17, 2018.

CHAPTER 30

Massinon, Stephane. "Police Uncover Four Bombs, Arrest Five in House Raid." *Calgary Herald*, December 23, 2008.

Martin, Kevin. "Real Honorio Sentenced to Minimum 16 Years Behind Bars for Role in Bolsa Restaurant Massacre." *Calgary Herald*, June 28, 2016.

Slade, Daryl. "Weapons Charges Dropped in De Winton Case." *Calgary Herald*, June 25, 2009.

Van Rassel, Jason. "Jail Term Hailed as Blow to Gang." *Calgary Herald*, June 16, 2009.

CHAPTER 31

Khatri, Yogita. "Bitcoin's Use in Darknet Markets Continues to Grow: Chainalysis." *The Block*, January 29, 2020.

Marinoff, Nicholas. "Crypto Criminals Rake in $4.3 Billion in 2019 So Far, Says New Report." *Decrypt*, August 16, 2019.

Orcutt, Mike. "Millions of People Fell for Crypto-Ponzi Schemes in 2019." *MIT Technology Review*, January 30, 2020.

ACT VI
2019 HIGH: $13,800

CHAPTER 32

Army, Scott. "Institutional Investment in Crypto: Top 10 Takeaways of 2019." *CoinDesk*, December 22, 2019.

Demeester, Tuur. "Bitcoin in Heavy Accumulation." *Adamant Capital*, April 18, 2019.

European Central Bank. "ECB Intensifies Its Work on a Digital Euro." October 2, 2020.

Kharif, Olga. "Bitcoin Whales Get Ever Bigger, Threatening Increased Volatility." *Bloomberg*, December 12, 2019.

CHAPTER 33

Di Iorio, Anthony. "Ethereum Cofounder Anthony Di Iorio Loves Decentralization — But Loves Running the Show More." Interview by David Z. Morris. *Breakermag*, November 9, 2018.

Köhler, Nicholas. "The Crypto King." *Pivot Magazine*, July 12, 2018.

Zak, Dan. "These Famous Men Are Trying to Tell Us Something with Their Retirement Beards." *Washington Post*, March 29, 2016.

CHAPTER 34

Ahonen, Elias. "Get Kieran, Paralyzed in Thailand, Home to Canada." GoFundMe, Inc., May 24, 2019.

CHAPTER 35

Cuen, Leigh. "Ethereum as Lifestyle Brand: What Unicorns and Rainbows Are Really About." *CoinDesk*, July 26, 2020.

Mezrich, Ben. *Bitcoin Billionaires: A True Story of Genius, Betrayal, and Redemption*. New York: Flatiron Books, 2019.

Orcutt, Mike. "Ethereum's Got a Hard Forking Problem Thanks to Another Delayed Upgrade." *MIT Technology Review*, January 17, 2019.

Spaven, Emily. "Bitcoin's 'First Felon' Charlie Shrem Begins 2-Year Sentence." *CoinDesk*, March 30, 2015.

Stempel, Jonathan. "U.S. Citizen Living in Singapore Charged with Helping North Korea Evade Sanctions." *Reuters*, November 29, 2019.

Weiser, Benjamin. "A Steppingstone for Law's Best and Brightest." *New York Times*, January 29, 2009.

CHAPTER 36

De, Nikhilesh. "Ethereum Dev Virgil Griffith's Attorney Files Motion to Dismiss Charges of Aiding North Korea." *CoinDesk*, October 25, 2020.

Marinov, Marin. "Winklevoss Brothers File Lawsuit against Charlie Shrem for $32M in Bitcoin." *Cryptovest*, November 3, 2018.

Ransom, Jan. "He Gave a Cryptocurrency Talk in North Korea. The U.S. Arrested Him." *New York Times*, December 2, 2019.

Zetter, Kim. "Bitcoin Exchange CEO Pleads Guilty to Enabling Silk Road Drug Deals." *Wired*, April 9, 2014.

CHAPTER 38

British Columbia Securities Commission. "Investor Alert: Crypto-Asset 'Smart Wallets.'" October 2, 2019.

BehindMLM. "Cloud Token Collapse Due to Hackers, COVID-19 & Authorities." May 6, 2020.

Cerato, Jan. "Calgary Man — Jan Cerato Well Respected Businessman Is Being Antagonized by the Lack of Fact Checking by the Securities Commission, Begins to Tell His Side of the Untold Truth." *The Life and Times of JantheMan*, July 20, 2020.

Giovannetti, Justin. "Calgary Officials Seek Source of River Pollution after Three Years of Elevated Bacteria Levels." *Globe and Mail*, July 19, 2019.

Redman, Jamie. "Cloud Token and the Rise of MLM Crypto Projects." *Bitcoin.com*, December 28, 2019.

U.S. Securities and Exchange Commission. "SEC Sues Alleged Perpetrator of Fraudulent Pyramid Scheme Promising Investors Cryptocurrency Riches." May 23, 2019.

ACKNOWLEDGMENTS

I would like to thank my editor and publisher at ECW Press, Jack David, and everyone else who worked directly on this book: Jessica Albert, Elham Ali, Crissy Calhoun, Sammy Chin, Emily Ferko, Jennifer Gallinger, David A. Gee, Jen Hale, and François Trahan.

I thank Rob Csernyik for both his feedback on the manuscript and meticulous fact-checking of it. I thank Leo McGrady for the legal scrub and Kristen Chew for reading the proofs.

My gratitude goes out to my agent, Rob Firing of Transatlantic, without whose tireless work and guidance this book would not be possible.

While this is my second book to be published, it is the first that I have written and was the fruit of the first deal I signed. I would like to thank Catherine Porter for putting me in touch with my agency, and for her invaluable advice on the publishing industry.

I thank those who've read the manuscript in advance and given me valuable insight and perspective: Harpreet Grewal, Nicholas Lim, Melody Ma, and Daksha Rangan. My greatest gratitude in this respect goes to Michael Allen, the first among the advance readers, who went above and beyond what was asked by looking over the book not only as a friend, but also as an editor.

An honorable mention goes to my girlfriend, Samantha. Not only was she an advance reader, she put up with my talking about this book for the greater part of three years.

Part of the book was developed at the Banff Centre's Investigative Journalism Intensive course, held by the *Toronto Star*'s Robert Cribb and Patti Sonntag of Concordia University's Institute for Investigative Journalism. I am forever grateful for that experience. Not only was the course crucial to honing the relevant aspects of the book, I also thoroughly enjoyed my time there. I thank as well the fellow journalists in my cohort.

This book would not have been possible without funding from the Access Copyright Foundation, for which I am grateful.

I thank Viviane Fairbank and all other staff with whom I have worked at the *Walrus*, which published my first piece of writing on cryptocurrency. That was a springboard of sorts for this book.

I thank the writers and researchers whose work I consulted, and the people in these pages who trusted me to tell their stories. Of particular note is Elias Ahonen. Over the course of the events in this book, we've become close friends.

If you've made it this far, please consider donating toward the treatment of Kieran Macleod, who broke his back on the Thai island. The relevant link is in the beginning of this book, after the title page.

INDEX

and pretrial conference, 176, 178
at Rodeo event, 134
at Rodeo lunch, 96
trouble for and lawsuit against, 134, 135–36, 137, 138–39
CBC (Canadian Broadcasting Corporation), and EL on Cotten, 170–71, 172
Cerato, Jan Gregory (JC)
and ASC accusations, 223, 224
ASC investigation, 146–47, 149, 152, 153–57, 159, 184, 185, 222, 229–32
ASC person at meetup, 143–44
at/and Bitcoin Rodeo, 126–27, 129, 130
birthday party of Angie, 85–86
and "Bitcoin Rodeo Supporters Lunch," 95, 96–97
Bitcoins as present, 97–98
and Blockchain Wealth Capital, 72, 74–76
blog, 39
change of fortune, 221
Cloud Wallet (or Cloud Token), 185–86, 187–88, 219, 223
company and services, 47
conference in Quarry Park, 147–48
description and profile, 46, 48–49, 71–72, 79, 128, 186, 223–24
EL's reaching out for book, 216–20, 228–32
and iPro workshop, 39
lawsuit from J. Ostrowski, 147, 149
legal issues about money, 150–51
Liber T Token event, 119–20, 122
Meetup.com account, 226–27
meetups at Cowboys Casino, 44, 46–49, 82–83, 87–88, 143–44, 149, 186, 187, 217–19, 226
mother's stroke, 77
note to L. Panneton, 149, 155, 156, 157
obsession with Bitcoin, 49
office and house, 71–72, 79–80
on own crypto business, 88
"private Bitcoin Investments club" and meetups, 82–83, 127–28, 159, 223, 224
promotion of Bitcoin and services, 126–27, 130
in Puerto Vallarta, 157–58, 160
RCMP and financial crime, 221–22
and regulation, 78–79, 82, 143, 222
retirement from cryptocurrency, 226
$60,000 incident with A. Jackson, 122–24
story in cryptocurrency, 216
and "whaleclub" investment, 79–80, 81–84, 86–87
China, 103, 109–10, 176–77
CIS (Commonwealth of Independent States), 167
Clarkson, Lannie, 48, 85, 86, 128
Clinton (EL's friend), 4–5
Cloud Wallet or Cloud Token, 185–86, 187–88, 219, 223
Coinbase exchange, 72, 224–25
coins, for oil, 68–69
Coinye West, 68
Consensus event, 96
Coombes, Angie, 85–86, 221
Corley, Eric (aka Emmanuel Goldstein), 210, 211, 212
Cotten, Gerald
alive after death, 168, 169, 171–72, 174
in cryptocurrency, 15–16
death, 164–65, 166, 167–68, 169, 171, 174

Jackson, Alex
    at Blockchain Wealth Capital, 73
    description, 47
    at Liber T, 122
    $60,000 incident with JC, 122–24
    and whaleclub of JC, 86, 128
Jake (seller of mining machines),
    42, 43
JanCity podcast, 144
Jaxx "wallet," 23, 198
JC. *See* Cerato, Jan Gregory
Joshua (friend of JC), 158

Karpeles, Mark, 10–11, 19
Kim Jong-un, 106, 113
King, George Clift, 27
King, Larry, 67, 90
Klein, Brian, 211–12
Klym, Jude, 150

Lee, Thomas, 131
Liber T Token, 119–22, 124
Longeway, Brad, 150–51
loss, in investment, 127, 224
Lou, Ethan (EL)
    beginning with Bitcoin, 4–5
    exchange platforms use, 162
    first article on Bitcoin, 5–7
    hack by Russian, 91–92
    housing as student, 8, 9
    impact of V. Griffith's arrest,
        213–14
    in-person sale of Bitcoin, 161
    in media about cryptocurrency,
        89–90
    meetups on Bitcoin, 38, 40–41, 87
    mining facility/company, 93, 131–32,
        161, 191–92, 193–94
    move away from cryptocurrency in
        2019, 193–94, 201, 203

offer of Bitcoin for Trump, 98
parents, 10, 12, 90–91, 103
path in life, 61
on personal wealth, 98
post-resignation and jetsetting life,
    90–91, 92–94
reaching out to JC for book,
    216–20, 228–32
second article on Bitcoin, 14–15
sources and research for book,
    233–35
trading obsession, 30–31
wealth from Bitcoin, 59–61
and whaleclub, 83
youth, 3, 53, 103
See also specific topics and people
LSD experience and purchase, 8–9,
    17–18
Luxx Group, 182

Macleod, Kieran, 191, 202
marathon in Pyongyang, 18
marijuana, and altcoins, 68
market prices, ups and downs, 131
Martin, George R.R., 131
Matos, Carlos, 37–38
Matthews, Kirk, 73, 128
McLeod Law, 155, 156
Meetup.com
    and iPro workshop, 32, 38
    JC's account, 226–27
meetups of EL on Bitcoin, 38, 40–41,
    87
Michael (Bitcoin miner), 41, 43–44
millennials, problems for, 9
miners and mining
    description, 40
    EL in mining, 55
    at EL's meetup, 40–41
    profit making, 191

ENVIRONMENTAL BENEFITS STATEMENT

ECW Press Ltd saved the following resources by printing the pages of this book on chlorine free paper made with 100% post-consumer waste.

TREES	WATER	ENERGY	SOLID WASTE	GREENHOUSE GASES
26	**2,100**	**11**	**80**	**11,130**
FULLY GROWN	GALLONS	MILLION BTUs	POUNDS	POUNDS

Environmental impact estimates were made using the Environmental Paper Network Paper Calculator 4.0. For more information visit www.papercalculator.org

This book is also available as a Global Certified Accessible™ (GCA) ebook. ECW Press's ebooks are screen reader friendly and are built to meet the needs of those who are unable to read standard print due to blindness, low vision, dyslexia, or a physical disability.

Purchase the print edition and receive the eBook free!
Just send an email to ebook@ecwpress.com and include:

- the book title
- the name of the store where you purchased it
- your receipt number
- your preference of file type: PDF or ePub

A real person will respond to your email with your eBook attached. And thanks for supporting an independently owned Canadian publisher with your purchase!